Sardinia:
Alghero &
the North

Eliot Stein

Credits

Footprint credits

Editor: Alan Murphy
Production and layout: Jen Haddington
Maps: Gail Townsley

Managing Director: Andy Riddle
Content Director: Patrick Dawson
Publisher: Alan Murphy
Publishing Managers: Felicity Laughton,
Jo Williams, Nicola Gibbs
Marketing and Partnerships Director:
Liz Harper
Marketing Executive: Liz Eyles
Trade Product Manager: Diane McEntee
Account Managers: Paul Bew, Tania Ross
Advertising: Renu Sibal, Elizabeth Taylor
Finance: Phil Walsh

Photography credits
Front cover: Faberfoto/Shutterstock
Back cover: Lpd82/Shutterstock

Printed in United States of America,
by Edwards Brothers Malloy, Inc.

Every effort has been made to ensure that
the facts in this guidebook are accurate.
However, travellers should still obtain advice
from consulates, airlines, etc about travel
and visa requirements before travelling.
The authors and publishers cannot
accept responsibility for any loss, injury or
inconvenience however caused.

Publishing information
Footprint *Focus Sardinia: Alghero & the North*
1st edition
© Footprint Handbooks Ltd
March 2012

ISBN: 978 1 908206 54 1
CIP DATA: A catalogue record for this book is
available from the British Library

® Footprint Handbooks and the Footprint
mark are a registered trademark of Footprint
Handbooks Ltd

Published by Footprints
6 Riverside Court
Lower Bristol Road
Bath BA2 3DZ, UK
T +44 (0)1225 469141
F +44 (0)1225 469461
footprinttravelguides.com

Distributed in the USA by Globe Pequot
Press, Guilford, Connecticut

The content of Footprint *Focus Sardinia:
Alghero & the North* has been taken directly
from Footprint's *Sardinia* which was
researched and written by Eliot Stein.

Contents

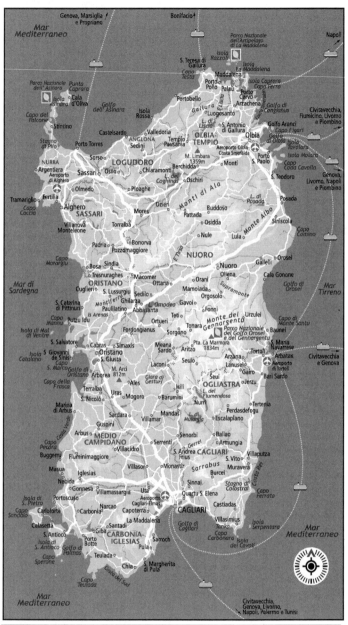

According to Sardinian legend, after God created the Earth, He gathered all the leftover pieces from everywhere else, threw them in the sea and stepped on them to create Sardinia or, as the Greeks called it, *Ichnusa*, meaning 'footprint'. Since then, the island has been walked on by anyone who has ever sailed through the Mediterranean. Invaded in name but never conquered in spirit, Sardinia has managed the clever trick of absorbing a cultural buffet of influences while holding its head high with a resolutely independent pride.

Lying 178 km from the nearest mainland, slightly closer to Tunisia than Italy, no other island is as marooned in the Mediterranean as Sardinia; a fact that has shaped the island's unique character. Although the Sardinians, or Sardi, have adopted the Italian tongue of their latest landlords, they cling fiercely to their native language, Sardo, and are recognized as a distinct ethnic group from their mainland countrymen, who drop anchor in droves each summer to splash around the island's beaches. Sardinia boasts the Romanesque churches, mosaics, medieval castles and fine wines associated with Italy but also pulsates with an unsullied and unscripted spirit that the mainland lost long ago.

Planning your trip

Places to visit in Alghero and the North

The Gallura

The northeast is best known as the location of the world-famous Costa Smeralda, known as the *Costa Rubata* (stolen coast) by locals. Developed by Arabs with Mediterranean panache, there's hardly anything Sardinian about this 55-km stretch of coast between Liscia Ruja and Poltu Cuatu, but it remains fabulous nonetheless. Pop Cristal with Russian oligarchs at Club Billionaire and tan next to football stars along the coast's kaleidoscope of shimmering beaches.

Elsewhere, nature has carved Gallura's coastline with deep, dramatic bays and sculpted its granite into supple, wind-whipped natural art. Nowhere is this more evident than around Santa Teresa, where spring erupts in a palette of wild flowers, and around the La Maddalena Archipelago, a national park of seven uninhabited islands with universal appeal.

Sassari and the northwest

Long before the Costa Smeralda was developed, the northwestern province of Sassari was the Italians' favourite Sardinian destination. It has all the trappings of the medieval mainland: a proud provincial capital, Sassari, with a corkscrew cobblestone centre and crumbling walls; the citadel of Castelsardo spilling over a rocky bluff, and a string of Romanesque churches frozen in time in the golden wheat fields of the Logudoro. But the region also possesses some curious cultural relics that could only be found in Sardinia. There's romantic Alghero, a piece of Iberia that sailed over to its seaside setting in Sardinia with the Catalan-Aragonese in the 13th century; Monte d'Accodi, a bewildering Neolithic monument resembling a Mesopotamian ziggurat, and Santu Antine, Sardinia's Sistine Chapel of Nuraghic engineering.

Nuoro and Ogliastra

To the east, the provinces of Nuoro and Ogliastra tuck their towns in to the craggy nooks and crevices of the Supramonte and Gennargentu mountain ranges, which shield them from too much outside attention. The tall massifs serve as a bastion, protecting some of Sardinia's ancient rites and traditions, which modernity has yet to sweep away. You can see examples of native costumes in the ethnographic museum in Nuoro. Elsewhere, Orgosolo is Sardinia's bandit capital, famous for harbouring and hiding outlaws in its mountainous folds; now it is equally known for the abstract murals on its cinderblock walls. Sardinia's two best hiking routes will take you deep into the island's interior: up to the mystifying settlement of Tiscali buried inside a mountainous sinkhole, and into the depths of Gola Gorroppu, Europe's deepest ravine. If you only have one day to stretch out on Sardinia's shores, take a boat trip along the Golfo di Orosei.

Best of Alghero and the North

Costa Smeralda Iron your Versace (or Levi's) shirt, wash your Lamborghini convertible (or Fiat) and head to the world-famous Costa Smeralda resort. This playboy playground isn't Sardinian but its faux-Arabian villas are certainly unique and its sparkling beaches are drop-dead gorgeous. What's more: you no longer need to be a millionaire to live it up here. See page 27.

La Maddalena Archipelago Unlike the Costa Smeralda, these seven dazzling islands sprinkled off Sardinia's northeast coast remain largely uninhabited and off the radar for European celebrities, with the exception of Italy's most famous warhorse, Giuseppe Garibaldi. Spend a day puttering from island to island in your own boat – or someone else's. See page 33.

Monte d'Accodi Climb the ramp to one of Sardinia's anthropological mysteries and archaeological masterpieces: the western world's only Neolithic truncated pyramid temple. Monte d'Accodi is a cross between a Mesopotamian ziggurat and an Aztec temple. See page 56.

Alghero Stroll the cobblestone lanes, try the spicy paella and whip out your Catalan dictionary in Sardinia's most attractive town. Four hundred years of Iberian rule have rendered this seaside settlement a virtual Spanish colony; its residents cling proudly to their ancient language and their newfound nickname, 'Little Barcelona'. See page 58.

Grotta di Nettuno Marvel at the stalactites, stalagmites, columns and fanciful colours in one of the world's great caves. Half the fun is getting there: visitors must come by boat from Alghero or descend the 656-step Escala del Cabirol! See page 63.

La Pelosa Wade through Evian-clear water at one of Sardinia's most perfect (and popular) beaches. While you're tanning, peer across the strait at Asinara Island, named after the world's only species of albino donkey. See page 64.

Castelsardo Blessed with a picture-perfect setting high above a rocky bluff, Castelsardo may be more gorgeous than functional these days. But thanks to its medieval castle, famous handicrafts and a killer sunset, you'll see why locals linger on despite the steep climbs. See page 65.

Hiking the Supramonte and Gola Gorroppu Lace up your boots to hike in the bald Supramonte mountains. Descend through a sinkhole to discover the huts at Tiscali. Nearby in Ogliastra, trek down to Europe's deepest ravine, Gola Gorroppu. See page 79.

Golfo di Orosei Explore this magnificent stretch of coastline which is also Sardinia's least accessible. For some 40 km, limestone cliffs dive dramatically into the emerald sea. There are no roads, so the only way to see them is to hop aboard a boat and cruise around for the day. See page 82.

Trenino Verde Pack a copy of DH Lawrence's *Sea and Sardinia* and pierce Sardinia's mountainous backbone aboard Italy's most popular tourist train. For five hours, the antique carriages plunge, climb and twist through some of the island's least explored and most stunning landscapes. See page 87.

Getting to Alghero and the North

Air

From UK and Ireland **Alitalia-Air One** fly regularly to Cagliari from London-Heathrow by way of Rome, touching down in Sardinia in five hours. **British Airways** flies direct from London-Gatwick to Cagliari between April and October. **Ryanair** run a brisk trade, flying from Liverpool, London Stansted and East Midlands to Alghero, from Edinburgh, Dublin and Manchester to Cagliari, and from Birmingham to Olbia. **Jet2** offers flights to Olbia from Edinburgh, Leeds and Manchester. **ThomsonFly** flies to Alghero from Birmingham and to Alghero and Olbia from London Gatwick. **EasyJet** goes from London Luton to Cagliari.

From North America The cheapest option from North America is to book a transatlantic flight into a European city that has discount flights to one of Sardinia's three airports (see below) – **whichbudget.com** or **europebyair.com** are both good resources. Note: you may have to transfer airports within the city you fly into and you should be sure to check the connecting airline's luggage requirements beforehand. The most convenient options are either to book a flight with **Eurofly** from New York into Rome, Palermo or Naples and take one of the many daily flights into Sardinia, or to fly with **AerLingus**, which has cheap flights to Dublin from numerous US and Canadian cities, and then hop on a low-cost carrier to Sardinia.

From the rest of Europe Flights to Sardinia from the Italian mainland are operated by the joint company **Alitalia-Air One**, **Meridiana**, **Ryanair** and **Volare**. Flying tends to be relatively expensive, with fewer flights outside the high season of May to October. The cheapest fares are generally found with Meridiana, Ryanair and Volare.

   Alitalia-AirOne, **EasyJet**, **Meridiana**, **Ryanair**, **ThomasCook**, **Transavia** and **TUI** have flights to Cagliari and Alghero from several major European cities outside Italy. **AirBerlin**, **EasyJet**, **jet2**, **Ryanair**, **SkyEurope**, **ThomasCook**, **Transavia** and **TUI** fly to Olbia. Check the company websites and **whichbudget.com** for specific routes.

Airport information **Cagliari Elmas Airport** ① *T070-211211, sogaer.it*, is 6 km north of Cagliari. Departures are on the top level and Arrivals on the ground floor, where you will also find a tourist booth and many car hire offices. There's a taxi stand outside Arrivals. A white or blue public bus departs every 15-20 minutes for piazza Matteoti in central Cagliari; buy tickets on the ground floor of the airport.

   Olbia Airport ① *T0789-563444, geasar.it*, is located 5 km south of Olbia and serves the northeast. This newly revamped, compact airport has a tourist information booth where you can buy tickets for the bus journey into Olbia (buses 2 or 10, every 30 mins 0730-2000). There's a taxi stand outside and car hire firms operate from a separate building.

   Alghero Airport ① *T079-935124, aeroportodialghero.it*, is 12 km north of Alghero and serves the northwest. This is the smallest of Sardinia's three airports. The Arrivals hall has car hire outlets and a tourist booth, where an assistant can tell you about buses into Alghero or Sassari. Taxis are parked outside and there's a private Logudoro service (logudorotours. it/orari.php), which runs buses to Macomer, Oristano and Cagliari; buy tickets on board.

Sea

The main Sardinian ports are Porto Torres (northwest), Olbia (northeast) and Cagliari (south) and the slightly smaller Arbatax (east) and Golfo Aranci (northeast). Travelling overland to Sardinia will involve a ferry crossing, taking between five and ten hours, from either France (Toulon, Savona, Marseille) or mainland Italy (Genoa, Livorno, Naples, Civitavecchia, Piombino). There are also services connecting Sardinia with Corsica (Bastia, Ajaccio, Propriano and Bonifacio) and Sicily (Palermo and Trapani). Note that some services from mainland France travel via a Corsican port.

While ferries to Sardinia take considerably longer than flights, they are usually more comfortable, with cabins and full amenities. However, with so many low-cost airlines in operation, flights are often the cheaper option. The cheapest and quickest ferry service from continental Europe is from Civitavecchia to Olbia, Golfo Aranci or Arbatax (4 hrs 30 mins, roughly €50 per person).

The French company **SNMC** ① *T0825-888088 or T020-7491 4968, snmc.fr*, sails from French ports. Italian operators (with UK agents) sailing from both France and Italy include **Grand Navi Veloci** ① *T020-8343 5810, gnv.it*, **Tirrenia** ① *T020-7244 8422, tirrenia.it*, and **Corsica and Sardinia Ferries** ① *T0825-095095, corsica-ferries.co.uk*. For more information on routes and timetables, consult the company websites or **aferry.to**.

Rail

To reach Sardinia by train, you can catch a fast TGV to Marseille from either Lille (5 hrs) or Paris (3 hrs) or a sleeper train from these stations to Nice, followed in each case by a ferry (see above). If you're travelling from the UK to France by **Eurostar** (eurostar.com), bear in mind that you'll need to cross Paris from the Gare du Nord to the Gare de Lyon to board the TGV or sleeper services, whereas in Lille all services use the same station. Alternatively, travel through the Italian mainland with **Trenitalia** (trenitalia.it) before picking up a ferry from one of the ports on the west coast. Whichever route you choose, allow several hours for a safe connection between the train and ferry. Buy tickets through **Rail Europe** ① *T0870-584 8848, raileurope.co.uk, raileurope.com*, or **SNCF** (voyages-sncf.com). For comprehensive information on rail travel throughout Europe, consult **seat61.com**.

Road

Car Driving through France to Toulon and taking a ferry for the 370-km passage to Porto Torres in the north of Sardinia is the most direct road route from the UK but will still take over 20 hours, including the ferry crossing. Unless the journey through France is an important part of your holiday, booking a discount flight and hiring a car in Sardinia is usually the more practical option.

Bus/coach There are no scheduled European bus or coach services to Sardinia but several organizations occasionally hire buses and vans for parties travelling between mainland Italy and Sardinia. Check nicosgroup.it, logudorotours.it and gruppoturmotravel.com.

Transport in Alghero and the North

Rail

In general, rail travel in Sardinia is inexpensive, comfortable and slow. Since train lines are limited, we recommend hiring a car to reach most destinations. A rail service operated by Trenitalia runs year-round, twice a day between Cagliari in the south and Porto Torres in the northwest (4 hrs, €16) with more frequent services from Cagliari to the main stations en route: Oristano, Ozieri and Sassari. Two comparable branch lines shoot off this route, one heading west from Decimomannu to Iglesias (40 mins, €2.80), and one east from Ozieri-

Chilivani to Golfo Aranci (90 mins, €5.65). Tickets can be booked at **trenitalia.com** or at the station via counter service or ticket machines. Even if you plan on travelling exclusively by train, don't bother buying a pass as a surcharge is often required, making single tickets better value. Remember, you must validate train tickets at the yellow stamping machines before boarding.

The **Trenino Verde** (see page 87) offers summer tourist train services along four routes that are slow but very beautiful: Mandas–Arbatax (June-September), Isili–Sorgono (June-September), Macomer–Bosa (July-August) and Sassari–Palau (June-September). Buy your tickets at the station before boarding.

Road

Car Sardinia's roads, when paved, are generally in good condition. However, due to the island's mountainous topography, few roads are straight and flat. Lanes are narrow, and dual-carriageways (eg the SS131) and rural roads are not lit at night and can be very dark. The SS131 is Sardinia's main thoroughfare and connects Cagliari to Oristano (1 hr), Abbasanta (1 hr 30 mins), Sassari (2 hrs 30 mins) and Porto Torres (2 hrs 30 mins). The SS131 shoots east from Abbasanta to Nuoro (30 mins) and Olbia (1 hr 30 mins).

Speed limits are 110 kph on dual carriageways and 50 kph in towns. Limits are 20 kph lower on dual carriageways when the road is wet. **Automobile Club d'Italia** (T06-49981 aci.it) provides driving information and offers roadside assistance with English-speaking operators on T116.

Many small towns have a single-lane main thoroughfare that has to deal with two-way traffic, so slow, cautious driving is recommended. Be aware that there are restrictions on driving in historic city centres, indicated by signs with black letters ZTL (*zona a traffico limitato*) on a yellow background. If you pass these signs in a vehicle, you are liable for a fine, although guests of town centre hotels are sometimes entitled to an official pass – contact your hotel or car hire company – that allows access to the hotel. Parking spaces with white lines are free, while those with blue lines require payment at nearby electronic metres, which are indicated with a "P" (roughly €1 an hour).

EU nationals taking their own car into Italy need to have an International Insurance Certificate (also known as a *Carte Verde*) and a valid national or EU licence. Those holding a non-EU licence may need to take an International Driving Permit with them. Unleaded petrol is *benzina*, diesel is *gasolio*.

Since July 2007 on-the-spot fines for minor traffic offences have been in operation; typically they range from €150 to €250 (always get a receipt). Note the following legal requirements: the use of mobile telephones while driving is not permitted; front and rear seatbelts must be worn, if fitted; children under 1.5 m may only travel in the back of the car. Italy has very strict laws on drink driving – the legal limit is 0.5g of alcohol per litre of blood – so steer clear of alcohol entirely to be safe. If your car breaks down on the carriageway, you must display an emergency triangle and wear a reflective jacket in poor visibility. Car hire companies should provide both of these, but check the boot when you pick up your car.

Car hire Hiring a car in Sardinia is a relatively hassle-free process. It's always best to hire with a reputed agency, and the least expensive option throughout Sardinia is **Thrifty** (thrifty.it). Other agencies include **Hertz** (hertz.com), **Dollar** (dollar.com) and **Budget Car Rental** (budget.com). Car hire comparison websites and agents are a good place to start a search for the best deals. Try **rentalcargroup.com** or **carrentals.com**.

Car hire is available in several town centres but better rates are generally found at Sardinia's three airports. You will probably wish to book the car before you arrive in the country; this is certainly advisable for popular destinations and at busy times of year. Check in advance the opening times of the car hire office.

Check what the hire company requires from you. Some companies may occasionally ask for an International Driving Licence, alongside your normal driving licence; others are content with an EU licence. You'll need to produce a credit card for most companies who will block a damage fee of €800-1,000 on to your card; this becomes unblocked if the vehicle is returned undamaged. If you book ahead, make sure that the named credit card holder is the same as the person renting and driving the car to avoid any problems. Most companies have a minimum age limit of 21 years and require that you've held your licence for at least a year. Some have a young driver surcharge for those under 25. Confirm insurance and any damage waiver charges and keep all your documents with you when you drive.

Bicycle Drivers in Sardinian towns and cities are unaccustomed to sharing roads with cyclists, so limit your cycling to the open countryside where roads are rarely busy. Bikes can be hired at many of Sardinia's major tourist destinations between May and September; prices vary depending on the quality of the bike but are usually under €30 a day. There are a number of companies offering cycling tours of the island.

Bus/coach ARST (arst.sardegna.it) and **FdS** (ferroviesardegna.it) are the island's two state-run bus/coach companies. The privately owned **Turmo Travel** (gruppoturmotravel. com) also has widespread services, while **FMS** (ferroviemeridionalisarde.it) operates in the southwest. Buses are usually reliable but are slow and time consuming. If you're travelling without your own vehicle, you are advised to use both buses and trains to maximize your chances of reaching a given destination. A helpful resource is **getaroundsardinia.com**.

Where to stay in Alghero and the North

Accommodation in Sardinia is varied enough to suit billionaire and backpacker alike. As the island has slowly awakened to its potential as a tourist destination, the range and overall quality of accommodation has greatly improved. Since the boom of the Costa Smeralda in the 1960s, copycat luxury resorts have sprouted throughout Sardinia, allowing upmarket visitors more opportunity to explore the island without sacrificing comfort. The latest trend in Sardinia's cities and towns is to faithfully restore antique palazzi and transform them into modestly priced B&Bs with old-world elegance. For those seeking something more adventurous and unquestionably Sardinian, no trip to the island is complete without spending at least one night in an *agriturismo* (farmhouse B&B).

From ritzy resorts to casual campsites, there are a few constants that apply to all accommodation on the island:
- Lodgings closer to the coast are generally more expensive than those found inland.
- Accommodation prices rise during the high season (July to September) and peak in the two weeks around Ferragosto (15 August).
- During July and August hotels throughout Sardinia fill quickly, so if you plan to visit during this period, book months ahead.
- Hotels and resorts that are popular often require a minimum stay of several days during their peak season; others may insist on half- or full-board.

- Those visiting out of season should note that many facilities shut down between late October and Easter.
- All accommodation requires guests to check in with a valid picture ID card; a passport is preferred to a driver's licence.

Resorts

Sardinia is home to some of the Mediterranean's most stylish and expensive resorts. From the Costa Smeralda and its five-star neighbours to the swathe of luxury getaways hidden around Santa Margherita, Palau and Villasimius, the vast majority of these pamper-palaces are built with real architectural flair and good taste. Just don't think about checking in unless you have a very full wallet: you may spend anything between €500 and €2,000 a night for a double in the summer!

Inevitably, the vast majority of Sardinia's resorts are built on or near the coast and come with private beaches. Most offer enough activities, such as sailing trips, diving excursions and windsurfing instruction, to ensure that their guests never feel the need to leave the resort's confines. A variety of restaurants is usually on hand, as are spas, pools and babysitting services.

Multiple options are usually available. Several resorts offer luxury hotel stays (Villasimius' Timi Ama and most complexes around Porto Rotondo and Baia Sardinia); others offer detached suite apartments (such as throughout the Costa Smeralda), and several offer guests the choice of both (Santa Margherita's Forte Village).

Hotels

In general, hotels in Sardinia are disappointing. Before the 1950s, the island's lack of tourists meant that there were very few hotels around. Most that you see today were built faily recently and suffer from the same lack of imagination that has plagued post-war architecture throughout Italy. While you will rarely encounter a hotel without air conditioning or private bathrooms, many seem outdated. If you do chance upon a hotel that combines character, class and comfort, it is likely to come with a resort price tag.

In Sardinia's cities and larger towns (Cagliari, Sassari, Oristano), hotels tend to cater to the business crowd. The closer to the coast you travel, the more hotels tend to resemble full-on resorts. Those located in popular tourist destinations are often affiliated with excursion outfitters and can organize day trips for you. A good resource for Sardinia's better hotels and villas is paridisola.com.

B&Bs

Where Sardinia's hotels are often modern, impersonal affairs, the island has a burgeoning selection of stylishly restored B&Bs that brim with character at a fraction of the price of larger hotels. Many B&Bs are tucked into the residential historic districts of larger towns or cities, providing an unbeatable location and an open-door invitation to live like a local for a few days.

Double rooms usually cost between €50 and €70 a night, come with their own bathroom, modern comforts and an invaluable asset: your host. B&B owners are almost always local, knowledgeable and keen to make sure you enjoy your stay in their town. It's rare to find a host who speaks polished English but with maps, a dictionary and a little patience, you may well find that they are a more valuable source of information than the local tourist board. Check out sardegnabb.it for a list of B&Bs around the island.

Agriturismi

You won't find accommodation that is more faithful to the spirit of Sardinia than the
agriturismo. An *agriturismo* is a working farm that takes paying guests. Visitors book
agriturismo because they offer an unparalleled glimpse into the island's authentic rural
heritage. With very reasonable prices and plenty of opportunities to get your hands dirty
on the farm, a good farm stay can be the highlight of a Sardinian holiday.

There are nearly 600 *agriturismo* in rural Sardinia, with most clustered around Gallura,
Oristano and Nuoro. Accommodation varies but most are more functional than fancy. In
some cases, guests live like a member of the family, stay in the guest bedroom and eat
meals at the family table. More commonly, guests stay in ranch-style detached apartments
clustered around a central building where meals are served. Rooms almost always have
their own bathrooms and, increasingly, air conditioning, but if you want luxury, this style
of accommodation is probably not for you.

Agriturismo are famous for their four- or five-course meals, so book a dinner when you
book your room. The owners often raise sheep, chickens, horses, goats and pigs by day, and
serve them to you as part of the evening meal at night, so you never have to worry about
the freshness. Following most meals, the chef or owner usually makes the rounds to ask
guests how they enjoyed the food. The website agriturismodisardegna.it is a good resource.

Campsites

There are roughly 100 campsites in Sardinia and most are by a beach. A basic tent
space with use of the showers and parking costs between €10 and €20. Some sites also
have hotel-priced bungalows and mini villas with their own showers and kitchenettes.
Campsites generally have a pizzeria, restaurant, playground and, often, a pool and are
practical ways to enjoy Sardinia's famous coastline without paying exorbitant prices. Most
are only open between May and October and fill quickly in high season, so book ahead.

Both campeggievillaggi.it/en/camping-Sardegna.html and campeggi.com are useful
links for campers.

Hostels

There are very few hostels in Sardinia and those that exist aren't usually found in key
tourist destinations. Compared to others throughout Europe, Sardinian hostels aren't
cheap (between €12 and €35 a night). Some hostels have an evening curfew starting as
early as 2200. Search ostellionline.org for a complete list.

Food and drink in Alghero and the North

Sardinia's isolation and poverty have combined to preserve the most distinct regional cuisine in Italy. Until fairly recently, most Sardi couldn't afford to import foods from across the sea so their tables did not feature Italian favourites. Instead, they depended on combining their own simple, home-grown ingredients. The result is a diverse regional menu whose highlights are not found anywhere else: paper-thin 'music sheet' bread, saffron-hinted dumplings, suckling pig wrapped in aromatic leaves and slow-roasted in makeshift underground ovens, and a digestive liqueur made from myrtle berries, to name a few.

Although surrounded by water, most of Sardinia's signature dishes are meat-based. However, as invaders, immigrants and tourists have come and gone, the island has absorbed outside culinary influences and has awakened to the mouth-watering potential of its marine resources, such as spicy Catalan lobster, mullet roe grated over clams and mussels, and some of the world's most sought-after tuna. Seafood restaurants have proliferated, especially around the coasts.

So, while you can certainly find pizza, lasagne, ethnic restaurants and Irish pubs in Sardinia's principal cities, if you're smart and just a little adventurous, you'll sample the local specialities.

Antipasti

Sardinian antipasti are designed to be a lighter preview of what is to come but as the portions are large, they can comprise a full meal. The most common starters are *verdure miste* (mixed vegetables) and *antipasto di terra*, in which salted sausage, *salame* and *prosciutto* are displayed alongside Sardinia's breads and cheeses (see below), often on a tray of cork bark.

Sardinia's most famous seafood ingredient, Cabras' *bottarga* (mullet roe), is served thinly sliced and drizzled with oil on bread. You'll also find *buccinis* (molluscs) or *arselle* (clams), served in a broth with parsley and lemon. Around Cagliari, *ricci* (sea urchin) and *burrida* (dogfish stew with hazelnuts) are also popular.

Bread

No Sardinian meal would be complete without bread and there are hundreds of different varieties. Each village traditionally has its own version, with additional loaves baked for special occasions.

The most famous variety is the *pane carasau*, often called *carta da musica* (music sheet) bread because it's paper-thin and cannot exceed three millimeters in depth. Dipped in olive oil and dashed with salt, *pane carasau* becomes *pane guttiau*. A thicker, rectangular and slightly harder version is *pane pistoccu*, a traditional shepherds' treat from the Sarrabus and Ogliastra.

Pane civraxiu ('chee-vrah-shew') is one of the island's most popular breads, thanks to its circular shape and dark, thick crust, which make it perfect for scooping leftovers from your plate! Around Ozieri and Gallura, *pane spianada* is a light circular loaf that was once decorated and served for feasts but is now eaten daily.

Cheese

Sardinia is to pecorino what Naples is to pizza and Parma is to *prosciutto*. Sardinia produces 80% of all Italian pecorino and the island boasts three DOP (*Denominazione d'origine protetta*) varieties. *Fiore sardo* is the most famous and has been produced by shepherds since long before they learned to make nuraghi. It consists of whole sheep's milk aged for four to six months in a damp place and often smoked over herbs. *Pecorino sardo* comes in two distinct varieties: *dolce* (sweet), which can be eaten a month after production, and *maturo* (mature), which should be aged for two to 12 months. Finally, there's *pecorino romano*, which originated in Lazio but is now primarily made in Sardinia.

Ricotta is one of Sardinia's best known (and healthiest) creamy cheeses and can come from goat, sheep or cow's milk. The three most common varieties are *gentile*, which is sweet and never aged, *salata* (salted) and *mustìa*, which is dry and smoked.

Pasta and first courses

The secret ingredient in many of Sardinia's distinct *primi piatti* is saffron, which is cultivated around San Gavino Monreale in the southern Campidano. The aromatic spice finds its way into Sardinia's two most typical first courses: *malloreddus*, which are dumplings rolled by thumb around a ridged surface and typically served *alla campidanese* (with sausage, tomato sauce and grated pecorino), and *fregola* (or *fregula*), which are small, circular grains of bran similar to couscous, best eaten covered in a sauce with mussels or clams.

Culurgiones are oblong ravioli rolled by hand. Around Ogliastra they come stuffed with potatoes and mint; in the south they're packed with cheese, laced with olive oil and sprinkled with crushed walnuts; and around Gallura they're made with sugar and traces of lemon inside a ricotta filling.

Maccarones de busa are common around Nuoro and are formed by piercing semolina dough with metal wire so that it absorbs the ricotta, garlic and tomato sauce that usually accompanies it.

Other mainstays are the Spanish-introduced *panadas* (fried patties) filled with beef, pork, boar or eel, which are popular around Gallura, and *cascà*, a Ligurian and North African-infused couscous variation served in Calasetta and Carloforte. Also good is Gallura's *zuppa gallurese* (or *suppa cuata*), made by baking a piece of bread with fennel, parsley, mint, basil and pecorino in sheep's broth.

Meat

Meat dominates the Sardinian menu. The island's most famous dish is also one of its best: *porcheddu*. A suckling pig is spit-roasted over ilex embers with a glistening of lard. In rural hamlets, traditionalists still dig a makeshift oven in the ground and wrap the piglet in leaves and myrtle berries to cook it, just as fugitive bandits once did.

Agnello (lamb) and *capretto* (goat) are often roasted with garlic, parsley and herbs, or made into *stufato*, a winter casserole with saffron, artichokes, eggs and red wine. If you're visiting Montiferru, try the local *bue rosso* braised steaks, which are some of the tastiest varieties in the Mediterranean. You'll also come across *bistecca di cavallo/asino* (horse or donkey steak) topped with oil and parsley. *Cinghiale* (wild boar) is commonly found in meat *ragù* sauces and at its freshest during the autumn and winter hunting seasons.

Fish and seafood

The best seafood is found around Cagliari, Alghero, Carloforte and the Sinis Peninsula. From March to August, *aragosta* (spiny rock lobster) is a common delicacy around Alghero, where it is served *alla catalana* with olive oil, tomatoes, lemon and a dash of spicy herbs. The Sinis is famous for its smoked *muggine* or *cefalo* (mullet), which produces *bottarga* (fish roe), while the Cagliaritani, dine on *burrida* (see *Antipasti*) and *ricci* (sea urchin) pulp at

Poetto beach each winter. Carloforte is one of the Mediterranean's principal tuna (*tonno*) capitals and serves its prized catch in a myriad of varieties (best in early summer).

Desserts

Instead of packing head-splitting amounts of sugar into their desserts like other Italians, the Sardi have fine tuned a simple mixture of eggs, honey, almonds, fruit and ricotta to form the basis of hundreds of treats. The most common restaurant dessert is *sebadas* (or *seadas*), made by frying a pastry filled with ricotta cheese and lacing it with honey. *Pardulas* are puffy cakes made from a fresh ricotta base into which saffron and orange peel are blended. *Amaretti* are sweet almond biscuits made from eggs and sugar, while *gueffus* are a mixture of almonds, eggs and lemon peel rolled into balls. *Torrone* (Sardinian nougat) hails from Tonara and is commonly sold at festivals. For detailed descriptions and pictures of Sardinian desserts, consult durke.com.

How to eat like a local

Sardinians have adopted the mainland-style breakfast, which is a quick, sugar-infused wake-up call doused with caffeine. Most hotels, B&Bs and *agriturismi* will offer a variety of meats and cheeses to accommodate their guests' diets, though locals do not consume such filling fare before noon. Instead, Sardi head to a bar or café, where they typically order a *pasta* (pastry) or *cornetto* (croissant) and down it with a cappuccino (strictly a breakfast drink).

Sardi generally sit down for *pranzo* (lunch) between 1300 and 1400, and linger at the table during their generous afternoon siesta. When lunching out, locals may order a main dish, a *contorno* (side dish) or *insalata* and a drink, totalling €15 to €25. *Cena* (dinner) is eaten between 2000 and 2200 and is a multiple-course, belt-loosening affair, consisting of mixed antipasti with bread and cheese, a *primo* of pasta or seafood, a *secondo* of meat or fish, and a *contorno* or *dolce*. It will cost €30 to €50, depending on how many courses you order. Most Sardi would never mix seafood with meat, though no one will bat an eyelid if you do. Top it all off with a *digestivo* and a toast (*"Cin-cin"*) – looking your partner in the eye as you clink glasses – and get ready for the *passeggiata*.

Wine

Sardinia's wines have long had a reputation for knocking out unsuspecting visitors. Italian poet Gabrielle D'Annunzio scribbled a lyrical rapture to his Sardinian drinking bender, and wine critic, Hugh Johnson, declared them to be "for the supermen [who built the nuraghi]". However, since the 1990s, Sardinian vineyards have started combining local grape varietals, diluting their notoriously high alcohol content and softening their sharp edges to produce sophisticated blends garnering some of Italy's top honours.

The following is a list of the island's best varieties, with a few suggestions for affordable bottles that are available at most supermarkets.

Red wines

Cannonau This strong ruby red is Sardinia's most famous red wine. Introduced by the Spanish in the 13th century, its full body matches well with meat and cheeses. The Nepente di Oliena is a wonderful choice, as are the Turriga and Costera varieties from Sardinia's top up-and-coming label, Argiolas.

Monica A drier red that turns purple as it ages. It was introduced by Spanish monks and goes well with fruit. Try the Karel cantina.

Carignano From the Sulcis, this is a sweeter choice in both red and rosé varieties. The Grotta Rossa and Nur labels are both excellent.

White wines

Vermintino Sardinia's only DOCG (*Denominazione d'origine controllata e garantita*) wine is this crisp, dry white produced around Gallura. It goes perfectly with seafood and is best from Sardinia's most famous bottler, Sella & Mosca. The Argiolas version is also excellent.

Nuragus This fruity blend has largely been replaced by Vermentino but Argiolas makes a quality version.

Dessert wines

Vernaccia A strong, sherry-like wine that goes well with *bottarga*. It is made around San Vero Milis in the west of the island. Josto Puddu has received recent acclaim for its varieties.

Moscato Made from Muscat grapes, this often fizzy and always-sweet wine is usually enjoyed alone or with fruit. Zaccagnini's Plaisir is pleasant.

Malvasia Introduced by the Byzantines and produced around Bosa, this strong, sweet wine hides a hint of almond. It's best by itself or with shellfish. Go with Malvasia di Bosa.

Beer and spirits

On average, Sardinians consume more beer than any other Italian region. The local brew of choice is Ichnusa, a pale lager that locals enjoy for reasons of pride as much as taste. For something with a bit more body, try Jennas, also bottled by Ichnusa.

The most famous after-dinner drink is *mirto*, a deep purple liqueur made by blending myrtle berries, alcohol and sugar to form what tastes like a delicious alcoholic cough syrup. It's best served straight-up but chilled. The island's potent *filu 'e ferru grappa* (literally 'iron wine') is made from grape skins and gets its name from the piece of iron that distillers used to stick in the ground when burying their hooch in the early 20th century to avoid paying taxes.

Festivals in Alghero and the North

More than 1,000 festivals take place in Sardinia every year (more than in any other Italian region), with many drenched in the influences of the island's past. Some traditions, such as the rural novenaria celebrations, hark back to the Bronze Age and are rooted in Pagan rites. Others are steeped in Punic, Roman, Byzantine and, above all, Spanish customs. Sagre (harvest festivals) still mark the passage from one season to another, and each town always honours its patron saint.

Most festivals, whether they be literary competitions, feasts or parades, are celebrated with traditional songs, dances and costumes. Rather than spectacles for tourists' cameras, these celebrations are genuinely local affirmations of Sardinian pride and identity: the essence of *Sardità*. Never turn down an invitation from a local to attend a festival: from town-wide processions to small gatherings in the woods, the Sardi are famous for indulging their guests and making them feel at home.

January
Festa di Sant'Antonio Abate (16-17th)
This celebration harks back to Pagan rites marking the winter solstice. Dorgali, Bosa, Desulo, Orosei and other towns pray to Saint Antonio for miracles and then light a giant bonfire in their squares. In Mamoiada, the *Mamuthones* awaken, while Ottana sees the *Merdules e Boes* parade through the streets in otherworldly, animalistic masks.

February
Carnevale (week before Ash Wednesday)
The central Barbagie continues its ghoulish parades, particularly in Gavoi, Ollolai and Orotelli, and daredevil horsemen race in Oristano's Sartiglia and Santu Lussurgiu's Carrela 'e Nanti.

March/April
Settimana Santa (Easter week)
Holy Week is marked by mock-funerals and silent processions throughout Sardinia, many of which still show the influence of the island's former Spanish rulers. Some that stand out are the Passion of the Christ procession in Alghero, where confraternity members don Spanish-influenced robes, and the Good Friday procession in Iglesias. Also recommended are the S'Incontru parade at Oliena, the Su Concordu Gregorian chants in Santu Lussurgiu and the Lunissanti feast in Castelsardo.

Sagra del Torrone (Easter Monday)
Tonara, Sardinia's *torrone* (nougat) capital, hosts a festival with plenty of samples and demos showing how the sweet is made.

May
Sagra degli Agrumi (first week)
Like a scaled-down version of Sant'Efisio, revellers parade through Muravera in costume to celebrate the citrus harvest, followed by music and dancing.

Novena di San Francesco d'Assisi (1st-9th)
Pilgrims arrive in Lula on foot from throughout Monte Albo, congregating at a Baroque church.

Cavalcata Sarda (penultimate Sunday)
Sardinians throughout the island descend on Sassari, where participants parade through the streets. The procession culminates with dancing. A horse race takes place the afternoon before.

June
Madonna dei Martiri (Monday after first Sunday)
Fonni's faithful carry a statue of the Virgin from the basilica through town.

July
Ardia (6th-7th)
Sardinia's bareback Palio-style horserace in Sedilo is dedicated to San Costantino. Spectators watch jockeys fly around a sanctuary dedicated to the local martyr as gunshots are fired.

Sagra delle Pesche (17th)
Little San Sperate marks its peach harvest by celebrating in its mural-decorated streets.

August
Is Fassonis (last Sunday of July to first Sunday of August)
Fishermen from around the Sinis Peninsula race through the Santa Giusta lagoon on *fassonis* rafts that have changed little since Phoenician times.

Sagra del Vino (4th)
Things can get messy at this generous wine-tasting gala in Jerzu, one of Sardinia's Cannonau capitals. Come well fed.

Time in Jazz (9th-15th)
Sardinia's resident jazz maestro, Paolo Fresu, returns to his hometown of Berchidda with an eclectic gang of world-class musicians to jam in the woods, on stages and in country villas.

Li Candaleri (14th)
One of the island's most colourful festivals sees nine enormous candle towers paraded through the streets of Sassari.

Madonna Assunta (15th)
Introduced by the Byzantines, the cult of the 'Risen Madonna' is celebrated throughout Sardinia when women in traditional costume carry a statue of the sleeping Virgin around town. The largest processions are in Cagliari, Orgosolo and Domusnovas.

Festa del Redentore (29th) Nuoro hosts roughly 100,000 spectators for its lively procession in traditional costume up to Monte Ortobene in honour of Christ the Redeemer.

Cabudanne de sos Poetas (end of the month) A literary festival in Seneghe, with poetry competitions as well as music, food and dancing.

September

Corsa degli Scalzi (first weekend) On the Sinis Peninsula, thousands of local men don white mantles and run barefoot from Cabras to the rural sanctuary at San Salvatore, 7 km away, to hide a statue of the Madonna, just as they did hundreds of years ago.

Premio Biennale (third Saturday) Ozieri hosts Sardinia's most important poetry competition in honour of Antonio Cubeddu, the local man who first organized the island's *poesia a bolu* competitions.

Autunno in Barbagie (September to December) This is an open-house invitation to see the traditions kept alive in the rural communities of the Barbagie. A different town hosts the event each weekend.

October

Rassegna del Vino Novello (early October) Milis celebrates the production of the season's new wines with one helluva party in its town square.

Sagra delle Castagne e Nocciole (fourth Sunday) You can smell the roasting chestnuts and hazelnuts from nearby Belvì at this harvest celebration in Aritzo. Folk groups sing and dance at night.

December

Christmas (24th and 25th) Many churches display elaborate nativity scenes and devout Sardi attend midnight mass. The day is usually spent with family.

Cap d'Any (31st) Alghero puts on a festive New Year celebration with fireworks above the medieval bastions. Other popular celebrations take place in Cagliari, Sassari, Olbia, and Castelsardo.

Essentials A-Z

Customs and immigration
UK, EU and US citizens do not need a visa, but will need a valid passport to enter Italy. A standard tourist visa for those from outside the EU is valid for up to 90 days.

Disabled travellers
Like the rest of Italy, Sardinia is a bit behind when it comes to catering for disabled travellers and access is sometimes difficult or ill thought-out. Contact a specialist agency before departure for more details, such as **Accessible Italy** (accessibleitaly.com), **Society for Accessible Travel and Hospitality** (sath.org) or Cagliari's **Associazione Italiana Assistenza Spastici** (T070-379 1010).

Emergency numbers
Ambulance T118; Fire service T115; Police T112 (with English-speaking operators), T113 (*carabinieri*); Roadside assistance T116.

Etiquette
Bella figura – projecting a good image – is important to Sardinians. Take note of public notices about conduct: sitting on steps or eating and drinking in certain historic areas is not allowed. Spitting in public is disrespectful. Covering arms and legs is necessary for admission into some churches – in rare cases even shorts are not permitted. Punctuality is apparently not important in Sardinia, so be prepared to wait on occasion.

Families
Whether for a traditional beach break or an afternoon in a gelateria, children are well catered for in Sardinia. The family is highly regarded and *bambini* are indulged. Do note that sometimes lone parents or adults accompanying children of a different surname may need evidence before taking children in and out of the country. Contact your Italian embassy for current details: in London T020-7312 2200, in Washington DC T202-612-4400, in Dublin T353-1-660-1744, in Ottawa T613-232-2401, in Canberra T612-6273-3333.

Health
Comprehensive medical insurance is strongly recommended for all travellers to Italy. EU citizens should also apply for a free **European Health Insurance Card** (ehic.org), which replaced the E111 form and offers reduced-cost medical treatment.

Late-night pharmacies are identified by a large green cross outside; call T1100 for the addresses of the three nearest. The accident and emergency department of a hospital is the *pronto soccorso*.

Insurance
Comprehensive travel and medical insurance is strongly recommended for all travellers to Italy – the EHIC is not a replacement for private insurance. You should check any exclusions and that your policy covers you for all the activities you want to undertake. Keep details of your insurance documents separately; emailing yourself with the details is a good way to keep the information safe and accessible. Ensure you have full insurance if hiring a car, or, if you're taking your own car, contact your current insurers to see if you require an international insurance certificate.

Money
The Italian currency is the Euro (€). There are ATMs throughout Sardinia that accept major credit and debit cards. To change cash or travellers' cheques, look for a cambio. Many restaurants, shops, museums and art galleries will take major credit cards, though a €10 minimum is usually required. Paying directly with debit cards such as Cirrus is more difficult in many places, so withdrawing from an ATM and paying cash may be the best option.

Depending on when, where and how you travel, Sardinia can be one of Italy's most expensive getaways or cheapest finds. Accommodation prices rise in high season (July to September), peaking in August. Hotel rooms average between €80-250 for a double and are more expensive than B&Bs or *agriturismi*. You can eat lunch comfortably for less than €15 and dinner for under €35 a person. With bus and train fares hovering at roughly €20 from one end of Sardinia to the other, budget-conscious travellers with plenty of time and patience can easily squeeze by on less than €100 a day per person. Those seeking to loosen their belts in style can spend upwards of €300, depending on their accommodation.

Opening hours and holidays
Most sights grant discounted or free admission to children, students or senior citizens, so always carry your ID. Stores and museums generally close between 1300 and 1600 for lunch and all day on Sundays. However, the main tourist sights in heavily visited areas are often open all day during July and August but may close down completely in the winter months.

Unlike those in Venice or Rome, most Sardinian churches keep irregular hours with long gaps between morning and evening openings, although, as a general rule, most are more accessible before lunch. (Where churches have fixed hours, they are listed in this book.)

Police
While it appears that there are several different types of police in Italy, the *polizia* (T113) and the *Carabinieri* (T112) are the most visible. The *polizia* are the 'normal' police under the control of the Interior Ministry, while the *Carabinieri* are a de facto military force. However both will respond if you need help.

Post
The Italian postal service (poste.it) has a not entirely undeserved reputation for unreliability, particularly when handling international shipments. Sardinia is worse. Passports are usually required when sending international packages (such as boxed souvenirs), and it's highly recommended that you insure your shipment and receive a tracking number. Overseas post will require *posta prioritaria* (priority mail) and a postcard stamp will cost from €0.60. You can buy *francobolli* (stamps) at post offices and *tabacchi* (look for T signs).

Safety
The crime rate in Sardinia is generally low, but rates of petty crime are higher than in much of the UK or USA. The ports around Cagliari and Olbia are reputed to be seedy at night but with common sense you shouldn't have problems. It is always advisable to take general care at night or when travelling: don't flaunt your valuables; take only the money you need and don't carry it all in one wallet or pocket. Pick-pockets and bag-cutters operate on public transport, so try not to make it obvious which stop you're getting off at, as it gives potential thieves a timeframe in which to work. Car break-ins are common, so always remove valuables and secure other luggage in the boot. Beware of scams, con artists and sellers of fake goods: you can be fined for buying fake designer goods. In general, don't take risks you wouldn't at home. Take extra care not to drive or act aggressively or to offend locals in any way in rural Sardinia – especially in the province of Nuoro. While banditry targeting tourists has vanished, the Nuoresi are not known for backing away from a fight.

Telephone
The dialling codes for the main towns on the island are: Cagliari and around 070; Iglesiente and Sulcis 0781; Oristano 0783; Bosa 0785; Nuoro 0784; Ogliastra 0782; Sassari and Alghero 079; Gallura 0789. You need to use these local codes, even when dialling from within the city or region. The prefix for Italy

is +39. You no longer need to drop the initial '0' from area codes when calling from abroad. For directory enquiries call T12.

Time difference
Italy uses Central European Time, GMT+1.

Tipping
Only the more expensive restaurants will necessarily expect a tip, although everywhere will be grateful for one: 10% is generous. You might leave a few spare coins at a café or restaurant that has provided especially good service or that has allowed you to spend an unusually long time at a table. Taxis may add on extra costs for luggage but an additional tip is always appreciated. Rounding-up prices always goes down well, especially if it means avoiding having to give change.

Tourist information
Sardinia's regional tourism office is located in Cagliari (viale Trieste 105, 070-606 7255, regione.sardegna.it, Mon-Fri 0900-1230 and 1530-1730). Useful websites include **ciaosardinia.com**, **hellosardinia.com**, **sardiniapoint.it**, **sardegna.com** and **sarnow.com**.

Larger towns generally have their own tourist office with English-speaking volunteers. Tourist offices in provincial capitals and popular destinations often carry information for the surrounding region.

Voltage
Italy functions on a 220V mains supply and the standard European two-pin plug.

Contents

Footprint features

The Gallura

Sardinia's northeastern corner, the Gallura, is a blend of wealth and wilderness. For 600 years it was the most impoverished and isolated pocket of Sardinia, until, in the 1960s, the development of the Costa Smeralda catapulted Sardinia onto the world stage. However, the arrival of the international jet-set created an island within an island, one that belies Sardinia's true character. While the Emerald Coast remains Sardinia's most famous tourist attraction, Gallura's charms lie elsewhere.

The region's proximity to Corsica means its culture is as much rooted in France as it is in Italy. In the 1700s, so many shepherds crossed the Strait of Bonifacio from the neighbouring island that Corsicans comprised three-quarters of Gallura's population. Many of Gallura's villages resemble Corsican towns, and the *Gallurese* dialect is almost identical to that spoken across the strait.

But it is Gallura's granite formations that distinguish it from the rest of the island. From the rias around Olbia and La Maddalena archipelago, to the boulders of the Valle della Luna and Capo Testa, nature has moulded Gallura's granite into sensual arches, striking columns and dramatic spires that rival the gorgeous beaches nearby.

Olbia and around → *For listings, see pages 39-47.*

The northeast's capital, Olbia, is a transit town first and foremost. Set at the end of a carved inlet, its natural harbour has always been the obvious point of arrival and departure to and from the Italian mainland, as the Phoenicians, Carthaginians and Romans all found. The influx of tourists flocking to the Costa Smeralda and surrounding resorts ensures that Olbia's port is the busiest in the country. Cars, trains and aeroplanes also converge on this overdeveloped town, creating a chaotic traffic pattern that has hidden much of its ancient charm.

Greek merchants called the settlement 'Olbios Polis' (happy town), leading many people to think that the Greeks established their only Sardinian colony here, but it is more likely to have been founded by the Phoenicians between the sixth and fourth centuries BC. Their successors, the Carthaginians, surrounded the town with towers and a wall (still partly visible on modern-day via Torino) in 350 BC before the Romans made it their most important naval base in Sardinia. After its brief incarnation as Phausania under the Byzantines, and Civita as the capital of the impoverished Giudicato of Gallura, Mussolini restored Olbia's Greek name in 1939. Since the tourist boom of the 1960s, Olbia's population has tripled, leaving its quaint historic district surrounded by causeways and construction but also ensuring it has plenty of accommodation and some great restaurants.

In town

Olbia's main drag is the pedestrian-friendly **corso Umberto**, a wide avenue running from the waterfront to the train station, lined with designer stores and cafés with outdoor seating. Beyond the Biblioteca Comunale near the harbour, a series of narrow alleyways shoot off from the corso into the town's compact historic district, offering a pleasant, if brief, stroll past shops and 19th-century homes. A right turn at via Cagliari takes you to piazza Santa Croce and the **Chiesa di San Paolo**, whose granite façade and belltower are enlivened by the tiles on its Spanish-accented cupola, built after the Second World War. **Piazza Margherita** is a good place to stop for a drink. Look for reminders of Roman aqueducts near the square.

The corso turns a bit seedy ascending from the piazza but turn right just past the train station onto via San Simplicio for Olbia's main draw, the 12th-century Pisan-Romanesque **Chiesa San Simplicio** ① *T0789-23542, daily 0900-1300 and 1600-1900.*

Around Olbia

Olbia's city beach is **Lido del Sole**, but a better option lies 5 km up the road at **Pittulongu**, a crescent-shaped strand with a sailing school and views of Isola Tavolara. (To get there catch bus 4 from the city centre or, by car, follow the brown signs north toward Golfo Aranci.) One kilometre before Pittulongu is Olbia's most famous Nuraghic monument, the **Pozzo Sacro di Sa Testa** ① *T340-811 9340, www.iolao.it, 15 May-15 Oct daily 0900-1930, reservations necessary out of season, €2.50.* Discovered by shepherds looking for water in the 1930s, the well-preserved site contains a large courtyard with 17 steps descending to a sacred well that dates back to 1150 BC .

Golfo Aranci

Continuing north around the Golfo di Olbia, you'll come to Golfo Aranci, the last affordable beachfront resort before the Costa Smeralda. This former fishing enclave has been expanding since 1882 when a track was laid linking its port with the national railway 18 km away in Olbia. Today, the town is really a sprawling collection of hotels and resort condos that descend past via Libertà's souvenir shops towards the train station and port, which has regular ferry services to the Italian mainland. There's an attractive seaside *lungomare*, with a playground for kids but, on the whole, Golfo Aranci's appeal lies in its proximity to 24 dazzling beaches that compensate for its lack of urban dazzle. The best is **Spiaggia Bianca**, a kilometre away towards Olbia, which entices a lively young crowd to its seaside kiosks.

Adventurous travellers should take the dirt road behind the train tracks as far as you can go, then park and walk 500 m to the twin coves of **Cala Moresca**, whose hidden beaches face the nearby **Isola Figarolo**. A 4-km dirt path behind the second beach leads to the wildlife preserve of **Capo Figari**, where a band of mouflons have thrived since their recent reintroduction. The path finishes with a view from below an abandoned lighthouse.

South of Olbia → *For listings, see pages 39-47.*

Beyond the concrete jungle of Olbia's suburbs lies Gallura's pretty southern seashore. From Porto San Paolo south towards the province of Nuoro, clusters of oleander and bougainvillea drape over holiday villas facing massive Isola Tavolara and its squat twin, Isola Molara. Unlike the swanky northern resorts, southern Gallura has been slow to awaken to tourism. The action does, however, accelerate in mid June, with late-night summer raves at San Teodoro, but slows again at the end of August, when these sleepy beach communities return to hibernation.

Porto San Paolo

The quaint beach town of Porto San Paolo has developed as a gateway to Isola Tavolara, which looms just offshore, and is a fantastic base for scuba diving and snorkelling. The surrounding coastline from Capo Ceraso to Cala Finocchio is a protected marine reserve that includes over 20 islands and rocky outcrops, plus two shipwrecks.

Two companies offer daily ferry shuttles between Porto San Paolo's dock and Tavolara during Easter and between June and September (every 30 mins daily 0900-1300, return ferries 1215-1830, journey time 25 mins, €12.50 round trip). Longer trips, with bathing stops at the crystal-clear waters of nearby **Isola Molara** and at Tavolara's eastern limestone walls, cost €25.

Isola Tavolara

The steep limestone stack of **Isola Tavolara** makes quite an impression as you approach it. Rising to 565 m at its peak, the craggy dolomite is visible well beyond the Gulf of Olbia, highlighted by a dramatic cloud that hovers above its crest, creating the island's own microclimate and, fittingly, resembling a crown placed atop the world's smallest kingdom (see below).

Boats from Porto San Paolo land at **Spalmatore di Terra**, a sandy tongue sprinkled with summer houses and two restaurants (including Da Tonino). The boomerang-shaped **Spiaggia Spalmatore** and its transparent water is Tavolara's main draw (for great snorkelling, head behind the pink house on the left) but be sure also to visit the nearby cemetery, where the tombs of the island's former kings are marked with a crown.

The world's smallest kingdom Giuseppe Bertoleoni was the first settler to arrive on the uninhabited island of Tavolara in 1807, intending to live there with one of his two wives after fleeing his native Genoa where he had been charged with bigamy. Bertoleoni soon realized that he was sharing his island home with a rare species of goat, whose teeth were dyed a golden colour by the grasses they ate. Word of these goats spread to Carlo Alberto, king of Savoy and Sardinia, who eagerly travelled to Tavolara to hunt the animals in 1836. Giuseppe's son, Paolo, guided the hunting excursions with apparent success, since Carlo declared Paolo the official 'King of Tavolara' on the spot and sent a confirming scroll a few days later.

The mini-monarchy was recognized by both the Italian king, Vittorio Emanuele III, who signed a treaty with the nation, and England's Queen Victoria, who placed a photo showing Tavolara's 'royal family' in Buckingham Palace, where it is still displayed with the caption, 'World's Smallest Kingdom'.

The installation of a NATO base on the island in 1962 effectively ended Tavolara's sovereignty and made roughly a quarter of the kingdom off-limits to the island's residents. Among them is Tonino, a 70-something part-time fisherman and the current King of Tavolara. When he's not fishing or transporting tourists around, Tonino rules over the island's 15-strong population, a few nimble goats, cormorants and a species of prickly knapweed flower found nowhere else on Earth.

San Teodoro

San Teodoro's natural setting tucked between a large mirror-like lagoon and several celestial beaches lends itself to tourism. Yet, it is only in the past decade that the quiet town has become one of the hottest summer destinations for Italy's vibrant under-30 crowd. The town's piazzas are lined with enough pizzerias, bars and discos to keep tanned young cocktail-seekers fed, watered and dancing well into the early hours. A quieter alternative is to stroll the town's outdoor handicrafts market, which is held each night from 2000 between June and September.

You can't go wrong at any of the town's beaches, but you won't find anything more stunning than the 3-km isthmus of **La Cinta**, which threads through the **Stagno di San Teodoro** (home to herons, gulls, flamingos, and other birds), and the shallow crystalline sea and powdery white shores just up the road at **Cala Brandinchi**.

Costa Smeralda and around → *For listings, see pages 39-47.*

From Porto Rotondo to Baia Sardinia, northeastern Gallura's glamorous beachside resorts represent some of the most expensive real estate in the whole Mediterranean. The Costa Smeralda was created by the Aga Khan in the 1960s as a clandestine playground for aristocrats and multi-millionaires. However, in recent years, the Emerald Coast has outgrown its 'exclusive' aura. As some sensibly priced hotels, restaurants and discos have sprouted up around this once-elite Babylon, models and CEOs now have to share beaches and dance floors with camera-toting tourists. Never mind the exaggerated prices and faux Arabian villas, the beauty of the Costa Smeralda's jagged coastline and emerald beaches trump its most beautiful clientele and you don't need a full wallet to enjoy them. A series of deep inlets divided by dramatically wind-carved granite is enough to make even the most jaded billionaire lower his shades in astonishment.

Porto Cervo

The heart of the Costa Smeralda is Porto Cervo, home in high season to mega yachts, plush villas and people who actually wear what you see on catwalks. For all the celebrity hype found in gossip tabloids each summer, Porto Cervo is a clever marriage of glamour and laid-back cool. It has enough flashy lights to keep you interested, at least for a day, although, if you come out of season, you'll find the scene is far more bare than bling.

Unless you arrive on your own boat, Porto Cervo first reveals itself along its **Passeggiata**, a pedestrian street lined with a string of cream-coloured designer boutiques where you can drop €1500 on a handbag. Make a detour away from the shops to visit the **Chiesa di Stella Maris**. This striking ode to North African architecture was completed in 1969 by Busiri Vici, and provides great views of the harbour. Its interior holds El Greco's painting of *Mater Dolorosa*.

A path leads from the church to the fan-shaped **Piazzetta**, overlooking the port below. This is the town's main hub and is thronged with yachties at dusk, who return from a tough day of beach-hopping to sip €5 coffees, €15 beers or €22-80 cocktails. Two stairways descend from the *piazzetta* to more boutique stores in the **Portico Sottopiazza**, from where a wooden bridge connects the town to the port. For a dose of culture outside the realms of Gucci or Fendi, climb the road away from the port towards the **Promenade du Port**, where two impressive art galleries have opened in the past year: **Louise Alexander Gallery** ① *via del Porto 1, T0789-92090, louise-alexander.com, mid Jun-mid Sep daily 1100-1300 and 1800-2400, free*, has presented work by the likes of Andy Warhol, Jean-Michel Basquiat and Roy Lichtenstein, while the **Monte di Mola Museo** ① *via del Porto Vecchio 1, T0789-92225, gocilgroup.com, mid Jun-mid Sep daily 1800-2400, free*, has the Moët & Chandon wine bar inside.

Don't leave Porto Cervo without taking a detour to its 720-birth marina, the largest in Sardinia. Set at the end of the resort's natural bay, this is really a sight to behold in high season, with 55-m yachts from all over the world bobbing at the quay, many with their own security guards outside.

Beaches south of Porto Cervo
The best bathing spots are south of Porto Cervo and are clustered close enough to let you visit them all in one day.

About 1.5 km from Porto Cervo towards Arzachena, the floury sand and light green bay at **Pevero** make it a favourite haunt for VIPs. Turn right from the main road towards Abbiadori and follow signs for Cala di Volpe and Capriccioli. **Liscia Ruja** is the first beach signposted and the largest and busiest in the area. The 2-km dirt road leading to its car park will seriously test your car's suspension but the narrow sandy strand framed by offshore islands is extraordinary. (Don't park along the dirt road or you may be fined.)

Leaving the beach and turning right toward Capriccioli, you'll spot the five-star Hotel Cala di Volpe and the Pevero Golf Club. A sign soon afterwards indicates a left turn to Hotel Romazzino, but before arriving at the hotel, turn right on to via degli Asfodeli to reach the coast's most renowned beach, **Il Principe**. You'll have to park and descend a lovely brush-lined path to reach this unspoiled gem. Back on the main road, a left turn leads to the twin beaches of **Capriccioli**, which are backed by juniper trees and offer one of the best views of the Costa Smeralda.

Porto Rotondo
Just down the road, Porto Rotondo isn't officially part of the Costa Smeralda but it doesn't deviate much from the area's theme… except that it boasts its own heli-pad.

In 1959 two Venetian Counts, Luigi and Nicolò Donà delle Rose, sailed their yacht from Tuscany to Sardinia on an underwater hunting expedition. Bewitched by the same shimmering potential for development that enticed Prince Karim Aga Khan, the brothers

From prince's playground to tourist theme park

Sixty years ago the Emerald Coast and its surroundings were little more than a swathe of *macchia*-covered knolls, lacking plumbing or roads. The area's only inhabitants, a few struggling shepherds, considered the arid badlands too dry even for their herds, and the deep fjords around which football gods and their wives now putter in their three-storey cruisers were once breeding grounds for malaria. The coast's fortunes began to change in 1951, when the Rockefeller Foundation recruited 32,000 Americans to spray 10,000 tons of DDT around Sardinia's coastal swamps, thus ridding this 55 km coastline of malarial mosquitoes and preparing the ground for a prince with a full wallet to dream up a jet-setters' paradise.

By the late 1950s, a few wealthy financiers had decided that Sardinia's hidden inlets and translucent waters made a great place to park their yachts. In 1962, Prince Karim Aga Khan IV, the 22-year-old spiritual leader of Ismaili Muslims worldwide and an international playboy, came to see what all the fuss was about. He fell in love with Sardinia's rugged beauty and convinced his high-rolling cronies to invest in an ambitious project to transform the barren landscape of the northeast coast into a world-class hideaway.

The Aga Khan bought more than 3000 acres of coastline from local impoverished shepherds at the equivalent of 150-220 a hectare and set to work. His Emerald Coast Consortium imposed strict building regulations, prohibiting the introduction of non-native plants and stipulating

that all water pipes and electrical lines be hidden underground. The prince hired Robert Trent Jones to design the world-class Pevero Golf Club, and top European architects Jacques Couelle and Michele Busiri Vici to incorporate the best elements of North African, Spanish, Italian and Greek architecture to grace the resort's pastel-coloured centre, Porto Cervo. The result is a striking pseudo-idealized Mediterranean village, whose petrified artificiality leaves nary a bougainvillea out of place.

The Costa Smeralda has not traditionally catered to Sardinians and has done little to boost their stagnant economy. The nightly cost of many hotel suites in high season tops the average Sardinian's monthly salary; many of the area's high-rolling vacationers never leave the confines of Costa Smeralda's private, foreign-owned resorts, and residents of its Moorish-kasbah-meets-Mykonos architecture turn up their noses at the Gallura's indigenous *stazzu* ranch-style homes. However, although this ersatz wonderland may be divorced from Sardinian culture, the Costa Smeralda does attract day trippers eager to spot or even mingle with a movie star. And, since the Olbia-Costa Smeralda airport was enlarged in 2004, new budget airline routes have made Italy's flashiest playground more accessible to average tourists. Sardinians, too, are finally benefiting from the influx: several locally owned B&Bs and *agriturismi* have opened in the area, signalling a new chapter in a prince's gilded fairy tale.

returned to Sardinia in 1963 with two suitcases full of *lire*, displaced some sheep and their owners, and got to work on what was supposed to be a few villas for their aristocratic friends. As demand grew, the brothers invited artisans to expand the resort, until their glitzy getaway was complete with six piazzas, arching bridges, Roman columns, the inevitable luxury port and private residences owned by the likes of Silvio Berlusconi, Shirley Bassey and Umberto Agnelli.

Like Venice, the village is closed to cars and has a central square named **piazza San Marco**. Just behind it, the rather ugly granite **Chiesa di San Lorenzo** houses 24 biblical scenes masterfully carved from wood by Mario Cerioli: don't miss the *Last Supper* on the church's right wall. Cerioli also designed the town's Greek-inspired granite theatre nearby, which hosts outdoor films and concerts most nights in August.

Baia Sardinia

The 5-km stretch of road north of Porto Cervo passes through soaring granite walls before reaching **Baia Sardinia**, often billed as the coast's family-friendly getaway. Prices may be slightly lower here but, aside from the Acquadream water park for kids (see page 44), there's little evidence to support this claim.

The community is centred around a predictably gorgeous beach looking out towards the La Maddalena archipelago. The area's main restaurants, hotels and shops are all found on the **Piazza**, which is designed to resemble a Mediterranean ranch-style compound. For wonderful views of the Costa Smeralda and unbeatable sunsets, head up to the **Battistoni** hill just east of the piazza.

Arzachena and around → *For listings, see pages 39-47.*

The entire Costa Smeralda lies within the territory of Arzachena, a former agricultural community settled in the 1700s by Corsican shepherds with a knack for making Vermintino wine. The town itself is a far cry from its plush coastal Mecca but a wave of tourism and prosperity has been blowing inland since the 1960s, leaving Arzachena's attractive centre suffocated by the sprawling development of retail stores and bumper-to-bumper traffic. Today, Arzachena's main appeal lies in its proud past. Five fascinating Neolithic monuments, including the two most impressive tombe di giganti in Sardinia, are clustered just outside the town, shedding light on the area's distinct 5,500-year history and culture. Nearby, the communities of Cannigione and San Pantaleo are an authentic antidote to the resorts that dot the coast: Sardo is still heard in the streets and things cost roughly what they're worth. North of Cannigione, a stretch of wind-sculpted granite rocks marks the way to Palau, gateway to the islands of La Maddalena.

Arzachena

On summer nights, when other Italian towns are getting ready for the *passeggiata*, Arzachena becomes a congested thoroughfare of commuters returning from the Costa Smeralda to more humble accommodation. Its charms are not easy to spot when you're crawling through the chaotic modern suburbs in first-gear traffic, but make your way up to Arzachena's *centro storico* and you're in for a pleasant treat.

In the middle of it all is **piazza Risorgimento**, a quaint square with a fountain and the elegant 18th-century **Santa Maria delle Neve** granite church. From here, go down via Ruzittu and turn left at via Limbara to reach the **Roccia il Fungo**, a granite rock that looks strikingly similar to a mushroom; it was used as a shelter by Neolithic tribesmen. A series of narrow lanes fan out from Arzachena's prettiest street, **via Garibaldi**, before dead-ending at 75 steps leading up to the **Chiesa di Santa Lucia**, whose panoramic views of the town and valley below make up for its lacklustre façade and bare interior.

Li Muri and Li Lolghi

① West of Arzachena, T338-378 7751, anemos-arzachena.it. 1 Apr-30 Oct daily 0900-2000, reservations required out of season. €3 for each site/€5 for both.

Head west of Arzachena towards Luogosanto for 3 km and follow the signs for the megalithic necropolis of **Li Muri**. Dating from 3500 BC, the site preserves a series of stone slabs fixed vertically into the ground like knives, outlining four circular tombs and one rectangular tomb. The tombs were originally covered with a horizontal slab and marked with a menhir, thought to serve as a tombstone or to represent the symbol of a deity. Though only small fragments of human bone have been excavated, the flint blades, oval-shaped beads and other offerings recovered suggest that those buried inside these single-chamber graves were the heads of a late Neolithic tribe.

Back on the main road, a right-hand turn leads to the massive *tomba di giganti*, **Li Lolghi**. As you approach on foot, you'll see 14 upright slabs placed in ascending order of height towards a central stele, 3.75 m in diameter, with a remarkable carved border. The small hole at its base served as a symbolic door to the afterlife. Behind, a rectangular burial chamber held roughly 100 bodies. In other parts of Sardinia, tombs were accessed from behind the vault but in Arzachena's tombs, the bodies were inserted by lifting the top slabs off the rectangular chamber. The frontal stones of the burial chamber were added around 1400-1100 BC and form a semi-circular exedra court, which was a place of profound cult worship. Legend has it that the area's Bronze Age inhabitants would eat hallucinogenic herbs in the exedra, entering a trance-like state that lasted for five days in order to communicate with the departed; a practice known as *incubazione*.

Coddu Ecchju

① T335-127 6849, legambientegallura.it. Apr-Oct daily 0900-2000; reservations required out of season. €3, €5 including Nuraghe Albucciu or Tempietto di Malchittu, €7.50 for all 3 sites.

Returning on the road towards Arzachena from the previous sights, signs indicate the area's most spectacular megalithic monument, the Coddu Ecchju *tomba di giganti*, dating from 1600-1200 BC. Located in front of a lovely rolling vineyard, Coddu Ecchju's two-stone stele rises to 4.04 m, making it a shade taller than Li Lolghi's single slab, and its burial chamber behind the exedra is better preserved. Like Li Lolghi, Coddu Ecchju's exedra was the setting for obscure rituals in which locals would place their leftovers in terracotta jars and smash them on the ground to wish their recently deceased relatives luck in the afterlife: a precursor to many modern wedding traditions worldwide.

Nuraghe Albucciu and Tempietto di Malchittu

① T335-127 6849, www.legambientegallura.it. Apr-Oct daily 0900-2000; reservations required out of season. €3 for each site, €5 for both, €7.50 including Coddu Ecchju.

At 3 km east of Arzachena towards Olbia, take a tunnel under the road to reach the two-storey Nuraghe Albucciu. It was inhabited from 1400 to 900 BC and lacks the distinctive cone-shaped design of Sardinia's usual Bronze Age towers. Instead, it's built on a horizontal plane around a granite mound. It's thought its maze of alleyways and barriers was designed to confuse its invaders; you can walk through its cool chambers and stairwells to its rooftop deck.

Take the footpath next to the nuraghe's car park and follow a dirt track for 2 km to reach the **Tempietto di Malchittu**, dating from the 16th century BC. The site consists of the remains of a stone wall, a large hut once covered in timber and a building with a small temple. Anthropologists remain baffled as to what exactly went on here but it's an eerily beautiful place with fantastic views over jagged granite ranges.

San Pantaleo

This delightful pint-sized town is best measured from end to end in human steps; rows of squat houses enhance its scale. Its dramatic setting at the base of towering granite spires provides a natural inspiration for the various sculptors, painters and craftsmen who have descended on the village since the 1970s, turning it into an artists' haven.

The long **piazza della Chiesa** is the centre of the village, where you'll find two art galleries and the lovely **Caffé Nina** (see page 43) facing the granite **Chiesa di San Pantaleo**. The main draw here is to stroll the streets, draped in oleander and wisteria flowers, and to dip into the art galleries sprinkled around town; among the more interesting are at piazza della Chiesa 1, via Caprera 18 and via Azuni 2.

Cannigione

Found at the western end of the deep Golfo di Arzachena, Cannigione developed slowly as a quiet farming community that supplied La Maddalena archipelago with food in the 1800s. Its main road, via Nazionale, wasn't paved until the 1970s and wraps around a series of pleasant public beaches: among the nicest are **La Conia** (look for a restaurant on the left with the same name) and **L'Ulticeddu**, past the village of Tanca Manna. The town is a less crowded base than Palau from which to visit La Maddalena; make reservations at the very helpful bi-lingual tourist office at via Nazionale 47.

Palau

The scenic road north of Cannigione passes through a dramatic landscape of wind-moulded granite formations en route to Palau. Located a stone's skip away from the islands of La Maddalena, Palau has long served as a gateway to the archipelago, with a ferry and chartered excursions (see page 45). Yet, it is also a classic beach town, with an attractive setting cradled around warped granite boulders, and recent luxury residential development has rendered it a prosperous resort in its own right.

Palau's most famous landmark is a 122-m granite block shaped like a bear, known as the **Capo d'Orso** ① *5 km east of Palau, T329-604 1373, Easter-Oct daily 0900-sunset, €2, €1 concessions*. Ptolemy used the promontory to help him navigate in the second century AD. From the land, you can't make out the form of a bear but a hike up to the beast's underbelly provides views across to the archipelago, especially in the morning.

Just west of town, the 19th-century **Fortezza Monte Altara** ① *T329-604 1373, Jun-Aug daily 0900-1200 and 1700-2000, Apr-May 0900-1200 and 1500-1800, Sep-Oct 0900-1200 and 1500-1700, €3.50*, stands guard over Palau and the offshore islands from a blustery rock stack. More attractive are the eye-catching views and imaginatively built villas scattered down the hill in **Porto Rafael**, a resort village that pre-dates the Costa Smeralda. From the small car park, head to the miniature whitewashed church and descend the stone path to a gorgeous piazza opening on to a seaside cove; it is perhaps the prettiest square in all of Sardinia.

Porto Pollo and Isola dei Gabbiani

Seven kilometres west of Palau, constant *maestrale* winds blow in throngs of watersports' lovers to the narrow isthmus separating Porto Pollo from Porto Liscia. This small point jutting out into the Strait of Bonifacio hosts the European Windsurfing Championships each summer and is scattered with outfitters offering kite surfing lessons, kayak hire, dive excursions and sailing classes for everyone from experts to complete novices. The rounded cape at the head of the isthmus is known as **Isola dei Gabbiani** (Seagull's Island) and is the location of Sardinia's most popular campsite (see page 40), which attracts far more tourists than sea birds.

Parco Nazionale dell'Arcipelago di La Maddalena → *For listings, see pages 39-47.*

The 63 islands of the Arcipelago di La Maddalena stretch north toward Corsica and are the peaks of a land mass that once joined Sardinia with its French neighbour. When waters flooded the Strait of Bonifacio millions of years ago, winds were channelled through the strait and any granite mounds tall enough to poke their heads above water were whipped into warped contours. The result is a marine playground that outshines anything the glittery Costa Smeralda has to offer. The archipelago was made a national park and marine reserve in 1996. Of its seven major islands, only La Maddalena and Caprera are inhabited year-round but daily boat tours allow you to putter to beaches on the other islands.

The archipelago's shimmering shores and strategic location have long attracted foreign attention. The islands were the first Sardinian territory to be disputed between Pisa and Genoa and were left virtually abandoned until Corsican shepherds arrived in the mid-1600s. In 1793, a 24-year-old colonel named Napoleon Bonaparte failed to conquer La Maddalena island, thanks to the actions of its most famous native son, Domenico Millelire, who hauled his cannon from peak to peak, firing at Napoleon's troops until they retreated. Millelire was awarded the first gold medal for heroism by the future Italian navy. More recently, the archipelago's residents have fought to rid themselves of a NATO base that occupied much of the park's territory (see box, page 104).

La Maddalena

Ferries from Palau arrive at La Maddalena town, a languid place of 11,000 inhabitants, where palms hang over prosperous 18th-century homes in eggshell-colours. A column dedicated to Garibaldi stands tall in **piazza Febbraio XXIII**. Two blocks up, **piazza Garibaldi** is the location of a lively indoor morning market and of the town's **Municipio**, which houses one of Napoleon's unexploded bombs. **Via Garibaldi** is the main shopping drag and affords prime people-watching from its many cafés. **Piazza Santa Maria Maddalena** is home to the island's parish church of the same name and displays two candlesticks and a crucifix donated by Nelson in 1805 in gratitude to the island's residents.

The town's waterfront offers plenty of options to cruise the archipelago by private boat (see page 45) but consider captaining yourself along La Maddalena's **Panoramica** road instead. This 20-km route rings the island, passing a virtual sculpture garden of bizarre granite shapes and stunning beaches, so pack a snorkel! Two kilometres east of town 'Panoramica' signs lead to the **Museo Archeologico Navale** ① *T0789-790660, May-Sep Tue-Sun 1030-1230 and 1530-1900, Oct-Apr Tue-Sun 1030-1230, €2.50*, which displays over 200 wine amphorae from a Roman cargo ship that sank in the Strait of Bonifacio in 120 BC. Soon after, you arrive at the placid (and packed) **Cala Spalmatore** at the end of a deep bay. Hooking around to the west, the larger twin beaches of **Monti d'Arena** and **Bassa Trinità** are popular with locals.

Caprera

A clanky wooden bridge connects the islands of La Maddalena and Caprera, revealing tall rows of pine trees and signs kindly asking you not to feed the wild boar. A left-hand turn at the end of the road brings you to the **Compendio Garibaldino** ① *T0789-727162, compendiogaribaldino.it, Tue-Sun 0900-1330 and 1600-1830, €5, €2.50 concessions*, home of Italian revolutionary Giuseppe Garibaldi, until his death in 1882.

Nicknamed the 'Hero of the Two Worlds', Garibaldi dedicated his life to fighting for independence movements throughout South America and Europe. Following the fall of the Roman Republic in 1849, he fled to Caprera where he spent a month hunting from a hut. He returned to the island in 1855 to build Casa Bianca, his home away from the battlefield, before leading his 'Redshirt' army in battles across Sicily and the Italian mainland – a campaign that paved the way for Italian unification.

Today the compound is a national monument. Inside Garibaldi's rather cramped house, visitors can see his trademark red shirts and his deathbed, preserved inside a glass vault. Outside are Garibaldi's grave and an olive press.

Caprera's relative flatness and shade are in stark contrast to La Maddalena, making it a wonderful place for cycling or walking. Among numerous footpaths, the best goes up to the lookout tower at **Monte Teialone**. The island's beaches are among the most renowned in the archipelago. A right-hand turn at the fork leading to Garibaldi's house passes the **Borgo Stagnali** and continues down a dirt road to the popular **Due Mari** and **Punta Rosa** beaches but we suggest turning left at the intersection and taking a dip in the sublime **Cala Andreani**.

Other islands

The five other main islands in the archipelago (Santo Stefano, Spargi, Budelli, Razzoli, and Santa Maria) are each worth a day trip of their own. Boats leave from Cannigione, Palau, La Maddalena and Santa Teresa di Gallura, or you can hire your own craft and splash around at your own pace.

The abandoned NATO base at **Santo Stefano** remains a military zone and much of the island is off-limits, though a private resort is set on the dazzling turquoise **Spiaggia di Pesce** (visible from the ferry between Palau and La Maddalena).

Most excursions stop at **Spargi** and, if you have your own boat, you'll want to spend as much time here as possible, since the deep inlet at the south of the island, **Cala Corsara**, is among the most photogenic spots in the archipelago.

The deserted islands of **Budelli** and **Razzoli** are marked by prickly *macchia*, fierce *maestrale* winds and rough bathing spots, with the lone exception of Budelli's **Spiaggia Rosa**. Named after its pinkish sand, the beach is among the most famous in the Mediterranean but, alas, has become a victim of its own beauty and has been off-limits to the public since 1999 because tourists started stealing the sand.

The needle-thin **Passo degli Asinelli** threads between Razzoli and **Santa Maria**, whose **Cala Santa Maria** is a must-visit.

Northwest coast → *For listings, see pages 39-47.*

Around the popular resort of Santa Teresa, nature has whipped Sardinia's northernmost point into a contorted jungle-gym of grey stepping stones, creating some of the best walking trails on the island in the process. This coast looks across the Strait of Bonifacio to southern Corsica, just 12 km away, so it's no surprise that much of Gallura's population and dialect are rooted in a shared history with its near French neighbour.

Santa Teresa di Gallura

Each summer, the modest 4000-strong population of Santa Teresa swells to 50,000 as vacationers descend on its attractive pistachio-coloured centre overlooking the sea. The town was founded in 1808 by Vittorio Emanuele I, who designed it as a 'small Torino', but, aside from Santa Teresa's right-angled intersections, it bears no resemblance to its Piemontese model. Much of Santa Teresa's present character sprang up in the 1960s during Gallura's tourist boom and its economy still revolves around the summer surge, with most hotels and restaurants only open from Easter to mid October.

The town's hub is the enormous **piazza Vittorio Emanuele I**, whose tourist shops and gelateria pulse with energy on warm nights. The streets surrounding the piazza offer some great shopping, and are an especially fine place to buy local red-coral jewellery. Nearby, the massive **Torre Longosardo** was built by the Aragonese in the 16th century as a lookout but now only guards **Rena Bianca** beach directly below, whose setting, hemmed in by coarse granite, makes it one of Gallura's finest. If you do nothing else in Santa Teresa, take the stone path from the right of the beach, which winds through a rocky wonderland covered in wildflowers each spring to a lonely headland with views toward Corsica's white limestone bluffs. One kilometre east of the centre is Santa Teresa's lovely tourist port, with its arching wooden bridge, from where ferries to Bonifacio and summer excursions to French islands in the Strait depart (see page 45).

Capo Testa

Of all the wind-whipped rocks strewn about Gallura, the crowning glory is arguably Capo Testa, 3 km west of Santa Teresa, where the *maestrale* winds have chiselled the entire cape into something resembling a cross between a Henry Moore sculpture and a Dr Seuss picture. One of the more pleasant walks you can take in Sardinia is the 3.5-km trail from Santa Teresa to Capo Testa (see below), especially in the springtime when the *macchia* turns into a sea of wildflowers (in summer, bring water and your own shade). If you can't get enough granite, head between Santa Teresa and Capo Testa to the beach at **Baia Santa Reparata**.

Santa Teresa to Capo Testa From Santa Teresa, follow the brown signs along via Capo Testa on foot or drive 1.5 km west along the same route and park at the small car park in front of a wooden 'Ente Foreste' sign. From the car park, a path descends through wildflowers and offers views of the coast (bring a camera) before reaching the sandbar isthmus that separates Capo Testa from Santa Teresa.

Climbing up the hill, look for the brown 'Colonne Romane' sign that leads to shallow Spiaggia Levante. From the shore, a stumpy column to the far left marks the Roman quarry where granite was extracted to build the columns on Rome's Pantheon. Snoop around these rocky building blocks and you'll find a few more Roman remains, particularly on the highest promontory.

Continue up the cape, because Capo Testa saves its best for last: a lighthouse built above a granite 'playground' that plunges into the crystal-clear sea. The area is ideal for scrambling and from the top of the granite piles, Corsica looks close enough to touch. If you show up at dusk, consider buying a bottle of wine from the make-shift snack bar in the car park, finding a free rock and watching the best sunset in Gallura.

West of Capo Testa

The coast west of Capo Testa is largely undeveloped. A strand of tall pines marks the *comune* of Aglientu, whose attractive **Rena Majore** beach is less crowded than those closer to Santa Teresa. From the beach car park, you can walk a scenic dirt trail for 7 km along the coast to the sleepy resort community of **Vignola Mare**, named after its Vermintino vineyards. Alternatively, the road between Rena Majore and Vignola Mare passes three more beaches found at the end of dirt roads (the bumpier the road, the better the beach) before turning inland towards a series of private holiday villas called the **Costa Paradiso**.

The ocean reveals itself again as you approach **Isola Rossa**, where crags shelter a tourist harbour and beach below a 16th-century Aragonese tower. This fishing town was founded by Neapolitan immigrants in the early 20th century and gets its name from the cluster of rocks visible offshore. To escape the crowds, head west to the 10-km patch of deserted sand dunes at **Badesi Mare**, where the surfcasting is said to be among Italy's best.

Interior Gallura → *For listings, see pages 39-47.*

Unlike Gallura's coastal resorts, change has been slow to penetrate the mountainous spurs that characterize its interior. The towns dotting these pinnacles are little affected by tourism and proudly retain Gallura's unique character, as handicrafts, not holidays, continue to drive the economy. Where granite permits, the countryside is awash in burgundy from the stripped oak trees of Italy's cork capital, and myrtle, cistus and juniper herbs lend their colours to Aggius' hand-woven rugs.

Tempio Pausania
The heart of Gallura and co-capital of the Tempio-Olbia province, Tempio Pausania was little more than a place to change horses on the road to Olbia in Roman times. It first gained significance after Gallura's coastal population fled inland to escape Barbaric raids following the collapse of Rome. When malaria decimated Olbia in the 1600s, Tempio became Gallura's capital for the next 200 years, only to see most of the regional authority gravitate back to Olbia in succeeding decades. Tempio's low-key profile has spared it from the sprawling growth that has affected its seaside counterparts and, like many inland towns in Gallura, it preserves a venerable granite *centro storico* similar to many Corsican villages.

Tempio's main promenade begins along **corso Matteotti**, where rows of cafés and designer stores entice pedestrian shoppers. A right turn at **piazza Italia** leads to **via Roma**; pop in to the shop at No 36 to see the world's only dresses made from cork (see page 45). The town's centrepiece is **piazza San Pietro**, where three churches are jumbled together in a cluster of granite and form the focal point of Tempio's poignant Holy Week celebrations. The most famous is the 15th-century **Cattedrale di San Pietro**, which has two wooden Baroque altars inside.

Past the stately **piazza Gallura** and *municipio* building on via Nino Visconti is the **Casa Nino di Gallura**, home to the last ruler of the Giudicato of Gallura (1275-1298), Nino Visconti. (Visconti was placed in Purgatory along with other careless leaders in Dante's *Divine Comedy*.)

Just north of town, you might spot locals filling up water jugs at the trickling **Fonti di Rinaggiu**, which is renowned for its therapeutic qualities. Far more impressive, however, is the **Fonte Nuovo**, set at the end of a park built by prisoners with views towards the dramatic peaks of the Valle della Luna.

Aggius and the Valle della Luna
Six kilometres northwest of Tempio, the delightful village of Aggius enjoys a spectacular setting at the base of serrated granite massifs where bandits used to hide. These days it's famous for being one of the last towns in Gallura where women still hand-weave wool rugs on a loom, a tradition that's fervently displayed throughout the town's warren of grey stone streets. To witness the weaving process and buy a rug, visit **ISOLA** ① *via Criasgi, T079-620299, Mon-Sat 0900-1230 and 1500-1930*, and **L'Albero Padre** ① *via De Cupis 11,*

T079-620196, Mon-Sat 0900-2100, where a family of women and girls weave the town's traditional designs.

Aggius is also home to Sardinia's largest **Museo Etnografico** ① *via Monti di Lizu 6, T079-621029, museomeoc.com, mid May-mid Oct daily 1000-1300 and 1500-2030, mid Oct-mid May Tue-Sun 1000-1300 and 1530-1900, €4*. Set inside a former *stazzu* (traditional *Gallurese* farmhouse), the fascinating museum displays regional clothing and agricultural tools, as well as an exhibit showing how various local herbs and berries are soaked in a cauldron for a month to create the vibrant colours used in the town's rugs.

North of Aggius' centre, past the picturesque pond and walking trails at **Santa Degna**, is the **Valle della Luna**, where nature has strewn colossal boulders to create an otherworldly lunar landscape; to explore, follow the **Panoramica** route by bike or on foot.

Calangianus and around
You'd never guess it from its austere exterior, but this humble town is Italy's cork capital; its wooded surroundings produce 90 per cent of the stoppers used in the country's wine bottles.

Cork is thought to have been harvested in Sardinia since Neolithic times and today it is produced in every region except Oristano. When the island's summer humidity kicks in, the bark of a cork oak tree loosens, allowing trained craftsmen to extract it with a hatchet. (By law, this process can only take place between 15th May and 15th August.) After nine or ten years, the stripped cork will have grown back and is ripe for harvesting again. Much of the cork is sold in its raw state and is used as serving trays for *antipasti* meats; cork for bottle-stoppers and souvenirs is boiled to render it more elastic. **Arte Sughero** in Calangianus has a good selection (see page 45).

Between Calangianus and nearby Luras, you'll see mountains of cork bark lying piled high as it awaits shipment. **Luras** itself is an attractive town with a fine ethnographic museum, **Museo Galluras** ① *via Nazionale 35, T079-647281, galluras.it, daily by request – phone in advance, €5, €2.50 children*, and four dolmen graves scattered around its outskirts: the easiest to find is **Alzoledda**, while the most impressive is **Ladas** (follow the brown signs from Luras' centre).

For something extraordinary, follow signs from Luras to **Olivastri Millenari** ① *14 km northeast, T368-337 6321, Easter-Oct daily 0900-1900, €2*, to see the oldest tree in Europe. Take a dirt road uphill towards **Lago di Liscia** until you reach a hut and three olive trees in a field. The youngest, a mere 550-year-old stripling is really just coming into its own; another is 2,000 years' old, while the third is (wait for it…) between 3,800 and 4,000-years-old and has a trunk measuring 11 m in circumference!

Berchidda
South of Monte Limbara on the main road towards Olbia, Berchidda is best known for its Vermintino wine, which can be sampled at the **Museo del Vino** ① *via Grazia Deledda 151, T079-704587, museodelvino.net, Apr-Oct Tue-Fri 0900-1300 and 1500-1800, Nov-Mar Tue-Fri 1000-1400 and 1600-1900, Sat-Sun 1000-1400 and 1600-1900, €3*. It's also the birthplace of Sardinia's most famous musician, trumpeter Paolo Fresu, who hosts the international Time in Jazz festival in the area every August (see page 18).

Monte Limbara and Lago Coghinas
One of the most rewarding outdoor excursions in this area is a day trip to the province's tallest mountain, Monte Limbara, and its largest lake, Lago Coghinas, a jaunt which can be tailored to suit the sporty and the indolent alike.

Travelling south of Tempio towards Oschiri, Monte Limbara's base reveals itself under tall pines. There are many ways to ascend to the mountain's summit, **Punta Balistreri** (1359 m), which is occupied by RAI satellite antennae. The most demanding option is to turn left at the Coradureddu sign, 7 km from Tempio, then trek along a dirt path up to **Vallicciola**, roughly 6 km away, before taking a paved road to the mountain's peak. The climb, from top to bottom takes roughly four hours, though the first part is a bit of a scramble. Less strenuous is to wind up to the mountain's peak by car: just past Coradureddu, look for a brown sign indicating Vallicciola. A third alternative is to park at Vallicciola and continue on foot to the top (1½ hours).

However you arrive, Punta Balistreri is a magical place, with sweeping views of the whole of Gallura. A few benches create a shady spot for a picnic, and there's even a small church, the **Madonna della Neve**. Don't descend without taking the stone path to the **Punto Panoramico**, where a statue of the Madonna holds the infant Jesus up to see the vista out to La Maddalena archipelago and Corsica.

Once you've regained your vehicle, continue towards Oschiri. After a stomach-churning drive through the **Passo della Limbara**, the shimmering **Lago di Coghinas** appears. You'll soon arrive at a bridge where the wonderful *agriturismo* **La Villa del Lago Coghinas** is located (see page 41). Drop your bags and take a dip in the outdoor pool, play a game of football, ping-pong or mini-golf, or, better yet, let Signora Caterina and her charming family organize a kayak or canoe trip on the lake for you. After a full dinner, loosen your belt and star-gaze from the terrace of your room: a modern *tholos*-style nuraghe built steps from the lake.

The Gallura listings

For hotel and restaurant price codes and other relevant information, see pages 11-17.

🛏 Where to stay

Olbia and around *p25*

€€€€ Gabbiano Azzurro, *Via dei Gabbiani, Golfo Aranci, T0789-46930, hotelgabbianoazzurro.com. May-Oct only.* Overlooking the striking Spiaggia Terza, this modern resort has fantastic views from its cheery pink rooms and from the poolside terrace. It runs sailing and scuba lessons and organizes horse-riding excursions.

€€ Hotel Cavour, *Via Cavour 22, Olbia, T0789-204033, cavourhotel.it.* If you can get past the wafting perfume as you enter, this friendly, centrally located hotel will keep you perfectly happy for a few days. The recently renovated rooms are all well insulated, refreshingly quiet and done up in soft colours.

€ Janas, *Via Lamarmora 61, Olbia, T339-109 2836, janasaffittacamere.com.* This charming B&B is tucked into Olbia's *centro storico* in an early 1900s home. Three rooms, two sharing a bathroom and each with air-con, look out onto a pleasant garden with lemon and orange trees.

South of Olbia *p26*

€€€ Hotel L'Esagono, *Via Cala d'Ambra 141, San Teodoro, T0784-865783, hotelesagono.com. May-Sep only.* Set around a lush tropical garden steps away from Cala d'Ambra beach, L'Esagono's rooms are spacious and full of character. The nearby summer disco is a perfect fit for those young at heart, but a drawback for those who like to sleep early.

€€ Hotel Bonsai, *Via Golfo Aranci, San Teodoro, T0784-865061, hotelbonsai.com.* There are no bonsai trees on hand here but the hotel does have a nice garden, a heated pool, Turkish baths and comfortable, if minimal, tile-floor rooms with good air

conditioning. It's a short walk from San Teodoro's nightlife.

Campsites

La Cinta, *Via del Tirreno, San Teodoro, T0784-865777, campingsanteodoro.com. May-mid Oct only.* Found steps away from La Cinta beach, this shady campsite has a modest market, five stone bungalows and is well suited to those who don't demand much in the way of comfort on a shoestring budget.

Costa Smeralda and around *p27*

Some of the plushest resort hotels on this coast (Cala di Volpe, La Bisaccia, Pitrizza, Romazzino and Sporting) are regularly listed among the world's best, with rooms that can top €2,000 per night in high season. For details see starwoodhotels.com, hotellabisaccia.it and sportingportorotondo.it.

€€€ Residence Rena Bianca, *Località Baia Sardinia, T0789-950060, renabianca.com. Apr-Oct only.* These pastel-coloured villas sprinkle the hillside 100 m from the beach, forming a miniature resort community with its own central square. The management organizes numerous coastal excursions including diving trips.

€€€ San Marco, *Piazzetta San Marco, Porto Rotondo, T0789-34110, hotelcolonnasanmarco.it. Jun-Sep.* Situated in the middle of the resort, this hotel has beautifully manicured gardens with a waterfall, luxurious rooms (some with seaside views), a pool with whirlpool spa, and a fabulous restaurant.

Arzachena and around *p30*

€€ Hotel Baja, *Via Nazionale, Cannigione, T0789-892041, hotelbaja.it.* Cannigione's newest and most luxurious hotel has the feeling of a Costa Smeralda resort without the heavy-handed price tag. There's a separate palm and rooftop garden, an outdoor pool and a beauty spa.

€ Ca' La Somara, *Località Sarra Balestra, T0789-98969, calasomara.it.* Nestled in a pasture between Arzachena and San Pantaleo is a converted stable with 12 rooms. Inside, the large hearth, tapestries and cacti give it a vague feel of the American southwest. The English-speaking owners serve hearty mainland Italian dishes. Burn off each meal with a dip in the pool, or ask about walking excursions.

€ La Quercia, *8 km west of Arzachena towards Luogosanto, T079-652302, turismolaquercia.it.* Even if you don't spend the night, call ahead and book a meal at this out-of-the-way rustic spot. It's run by a young couple who cook up *Gallurese* favourites fused with recipes from their native Iglesiente. The results are so delicious and abundant, you'll want to book one of the modest rooms and pass out.

€ Rena, *Località Rena, 3 km north of Arzachena, T0789-82532, agriturismorena. it.* This *agriturismo* is located in a converted *stazzu*, owned by the English-speaking Ruzittu family. Juniper beams preside over a fireplace and wooden rooms have views out to fields with cork and olive trees. Purchase farm honey and ham, and don't miss the bountiful dinner!

€ S'Olias, *Località Ancioggiu, Cannigione, T0789-88303, solias.it.* This revamped granite *stazzu*-style house is set in a large pasture dotted with olive trees and feels a lot more like an *agriturismo* than a hotel. The 10 rooms each have air conditioning, comfy beds and terraces leading out to the green surroundings. Dinners are served in a stone dining room.

€ Tenuta Pilastru, *Località Pilastru, 5 km west of Arzachena, T0789-82936, tenutapilastru.it.* Thirty-two *stazzu*-style cottages are sprinkled throughout a granite wonderland bordered by livestock pastures at this impressive *agriturismo*. Each room has satellite TV and air conditioning. The wines are home-produced and the *zuppa gallurese* is sensational.

Campsites

Campeggio Isola dei Gabbiani, *Località Isola dei Gabbiani, T0789-704019, isoladeigabbiani.it. Mid Mar-Oct only.* Occupying the entire 18-ha island, this site is a village unto itself with bars, a disco, restaurant and its own windsurfing school. Your best bet is to stay in one of the wind-resistant bungalows.

Capo d'Orso, *Località Golfo delle Saline, Palau, T0789-702007, capodorso.it. Jun-Sep only.* This camping village has bungalows and cottages, as well as spaces for camper vans and tents. The site is found directly on the placid Golfo delle Saline beach and boasts its own dive centre, football and tennis courts.

Golfo di Arzachena, *main road between Arzachena and Cannigione, T0789-88101, campingarzachena.com. Mar-Oct only.* You won't find a cheaper deal this close to the Costa Smeralda. The campsite's large pool, air-conditioned apartments, games room and pizzeria make for a pleasant stay surrounded by world-class luxury.

Parco Nazionale dell'Arcipelago di La Maddalena *p33*

€€€ Cala Lunga, *Località Porto Massimo, La Maddalena, T0789-794001, hotelcalalunga. com. Jun-Sep only.* Found 15 minutes from town among La Maddalena's poshest resorts. The 74 rooms are modern with a seaside view. Relax in the pool, rent scuba gear and scooters, or tour the coast from the resort's own port.

€€ Miralonga, *Via Don Vico, La Maddalena, T0789-722563, miralonga.it.* This modern-looking cream hotel is set just off the Strada Panoramica. The functional rooms have balconies facing an attractive bay. A decent restaurant serves good seafood next to the hotel's square swimming pool. The diving centre by the shore is a plus.

€€ Sa Bertula, *Via Indipendenza, La Maddalena, T0789-727425, sabertula.com.* Colourfully painted *murales* enliven the atmosphere of this country-style B&B. The three rooms each have en suite facilities and air conditioning.

Northwest coast *p34*

€€€ Hotel Corallaro, *Rena Bianca, Santa Teresa di Gallura, T0789-755431, hotelcorallaro.it. May-Sep only*. You won't get any closer to the beach than in this complex overlooking Corsica. Private boat excursions, an indoor and outdoor pool, satellite televisions and a Turkish bath make this Santa Teresa's most chi-chi option. Most rooms have balconies and those facing the sea have top-notch views.

€€ Hotel Moderno, *Via Umberto 39, Santa Teresa di Gallura, T0789-754233, modernoweb.it. Apr-Sep*. This *centralissimo* hotel is run by a charming woman from Genoa. The top rooms have their own balcony offering wonderful rooftop views across town. The decor throughout has an attractive traditional motif with classic Sardinian animal designs in lively colours.

Interior Gallura *p36*

€€ L'Agnata, *Località l'Agnata, between Tempio Pausania and Oschiri, T079-671384, agnata.it*. In the middle of a 6.5 km road leading nowhere is Sardinia's most famous and luxurious *agriturismo*, created by the Italian singer, Fabrizio de André, in 1973. Grapes dangle above as you approach the getaway's ivy-covered centrepiece: an elliptical pool ringed by granite rocks. Around it are the cosy rooms, each with balconies and oak chests. There's no working farm here but there are enough cats to convey a rural feeling, and the exquisite cuisine is a sophisticated arrangement of *Gallurese* delicacies.

€€ Petit Hotel, *Piazza De Gasperi 9/11, Tempio Pausania, T079-631134, petit-hotel. it*. This hotel's austere exterior belies its warm furnishings. Inside, French doors and wooden trimmings abound and the rooms are quite spacious, with dramatic views from the back toward Aggius' granite mountains.

€ Il Muto di Gallura, *Località Fraiga, 1 km from Aggius, T079-620559, mutodigallura. com*. Named after a famous bandit, this *agriturismo* remains a working *stazzu* where donkeys, sheep and cows are bred to make the farm self-sufficient. There's an outdoor pool and horseriding is available, or you can try your luck hunting quail or wild boar. Rooms have modern conveniences and dinners come with home-produced wine.

€ La Villa del Lago Coghinas, *Località Mandras, Oschiri, T338-7145131, riturismovilladellagocoghinas.it*. This charming *agriturismo* on the shores of Lake Coghinas is an outdoor lover's paradise. Bring your own gear and fish in the lake, bike through the mountains or trek around the hillsides. The farmhouse has an outdoor pool, ping-pong, mini-golf, football, and can organize excursions around the lake by boat. At dinner, Signora Caterina prepares *malloreddus*, kid or suckling pig.

🍴 Restaurants

Olbia and around *p25*

€€€€ Gallura, *Corso Umberto 145, Olbia, T0789-24648. Tue-Sun 2000-2230*. One of Sardinia's, if not Italy's, best restaurants. Owner and head chef Rita Denza has been cooking *Gallurese* specialities since the 1940s and adds a unique creativity to traditional classics. Her pasta dishes with sage and saffron are extraordinary, and she recommends that her diners choose their *secondi* based on the seasons: mussels or goat with olives in summer, Gallura's famous *mazzafrissa* (semolina pasta with cream) in autumn, and lamb during the winter.

€€€€ Miramare, *Piazza del Porto 2, Golfo Aranci, T0789-46085. Sat-Thu 1930-2300*. Located right on the port, this was the first restaurant in town and still serves the area's best seafood nearly 100 years later. Sit under the veranda to taste the mussels filled with mortadella, or the subtle octopus, and ask for the house Vermintino wine.

€€€ Da Bartolo, *Via Aldo Moro 133, Olbia, T0789-51348. May-Oct daily 1930-2230, Nov-Apr Mon-Sat 1930-2230.* Located inside the Stella 2000 hotel, Da Bartolo is well respected for its fresh fish courses. Call ahead for the spicy lobster *a la catalana*, or show up and try the more subtle spaghetti with sea urchin.

€€ La Lanterna, *Via Olbia 13, Olbia, T0789-23082. May-Oct daily 1930-2230, Nov-Apr Thu-Tue 1930-2230.* Set in one of Olbia's quaint narrow alleys, La Lanterna serves up enormous steaks, tasty pizzas and beautifully presented seafood . The *baccalà* is especially good, as are the lemon-scented ravioli stuffed with ricotta.

Cafés and bars
Café Mary, *Piazza Regina Margherita 10, Olbia, T0789-608005. Daily 0700-0200.* A popular people-watching spot at the corner of Olbia's *passeggiata* thoroughfare.

South of Olbia *p26*
€€€ Da Tonino, *Località Isola Tavolara, T0789-58570. Easter-Oct daily 1100-2200.* Tavolara's king, Tonino, runs this pricey but yummy seafood restaurant on Spalmatore beach; his sister runs the island's other restaurant. Go for the novelty, but stay for the seaside views, fresh clams and well-cooked fish.

€€€ Il Covo, *Località Puntaldia, 8 km north of San Teodoro, T0784-863043. Apr-Sep daily 1900-2400.* Head here for a break from San Teodoro's string of pizzerias and sample the area's best seafood. The lobster and clams are both tasty.

Cafés and bars
Café Florian, *Via Sardegna 5, San Teodoro. Tue-Sun 0800-0200.* Serves salads, bruschetta, cocktails and gelato in an art nouveau setting.

Costa Smeralda and around *p27*
€€€€ Lu Stazzu, *Località Monte Ladu, Porto Rotondo, T0789-34837. Easter-Oct daily 1930-2300.* Porto Rotondo's best restaurant is located about 1 km outside the centre in a converted *stazzu*. Sit back as waiters serve you with trays of traditional Sardinian cuisine. Fixed menu €40.

€€€€ Ristorante Yacht Club, *Via della Marina, Porto Cervo, T0789-902200. May-Sep only.* People take themselves pretty seriously here. Dine outdoors facing some of the largest yachts you've ever seen while peering over at their owners next to you. The seafood cuisine is delicious and outrageously expensive.

€€€ Ristorante Pomodoro, *Piazza Cervo, Porto Cervo, T0789-931626. Mon-Fri 1900-2300.* Pizzas from €10, tasty shellfish, good local cheeses and romantic outdoor seating add up to the best-value dining on the Costa Smeralda.

Cafés and bars
Pina Colada Bar, *Portico Sottopiazza, Porto Cervo. Jun-early Sep daily 1100-2400.* Porto Cervo's discount bar-café keeps plenty of wine on ice and has €5 panini.

Arzachena and around *p30*
€€€ Agriturismo La Colti, *between Arzachena and Cannigione, T0789-88440. Apr-early Nov daily, dinner only, reservations essential.* This converted granite *stazzu* sits on an enormous 120-ha lot among rolling hills. Inside, the beautifully displayed agricultural tools are reminiscent of an ethnographic museum. Dine on typical *Gallurese suppa cuata* (Gallura's version of lasagne, made with pecorino, broth and bread), *mazzafrissa* (semolina pasta with cream) and the award-winning pigs and cows that are bred outside. Fixed menu €30.

€€€ Da Franco, *Via Capo d'Orso 1, Palau, T0789-709558. Tue-Sun 1230-1430 and 1900-2330.* Palau's best restaurant was opened in 1961 by Salvatore Malu; his grandson, Alessandro, now carries on the family tradition. This elegant establishment has Murano lamps and stiff tablecloths to accompany the fresh fish bought daily from the market. The prawns in a ginger cream are excellent, as is the *zuppa arcipelago*: a soup of fish and shellfish.

€€€ *La Vecchia Arzachena*, *Via Garibaldi 15b, Arzachena, T0789-83105. Mon-Sat 1230-1500 and 1900-2300, Sun 1900-2300.* This attractive restaurant's two rooms are awash with opulent ceiling murals under which waiters flit back and forth efficiently. Choose from seafood or meat dishes, among which the tagliatelle in a tomato sauce is delicious. Regulars recommend the fish of the day.

€€€ Ristorante del Porto, *Via Nazionale 94, Cannigione, T0789-88011. Easter-Oct daily 1300-1530 and 2000-2200.* Inside the hotel of the same name, this restaurant has been in the same hands for over 50 years and is a Cannigione staple. A fine wine list complements well-prepared seafood dishes, such as local lobster and sea urchins, prepared by Bartolomeo and Bastiana.

Cafés and bars
Caffè Nina, *Piazzetta San Pantaleo, San Pantaleo, T338-368 7288. May-Oct daily 0900-0230.* This cutesy café in the middle of the town's art scene has pleasant outdoor seating facing the granite church.

Parco Nazionale dell'Arcipelago di La Maddalena *p33*
€€€ Perla Blu, *Piazza Barone des Geneys, La Maddalena, T0789-735373. Wed-Mon 1230-1500 and 1930-2230.* The restaurant's terrace seating overlooks La Maddalena's port and is conveniently located next to the tourist office. Locals slurp up mussels and pick their fish bones dry. Try the ravioli stuffed with fish and pesto.

€€ Garibaldi, *800 m after bridge, Caprera, T0789-727449. Lunch and dinner by reservation.* This *agriturismo* is surrounded by potted flowers and run by a couple from Nuoro who make their own pecorino and ricotta cheeses from the farm's sheep. Come hungry and prepare to eat a four-

course meal topped off with a shot of homemade *mirto*. (€23 lunch, €30 dinner).

Northwest coast *p34*
€€€€ Riva, *Via del Porto 29, Santa Teresa di Gallura, T347-294 8196. Easter-Oct Thu-Tue 1930-2330.* Owner Vittorio Riva is among Santa Teresa's most highly-regarded seafood connoisseurs. Inside the warm, yellow restaurant, try the spaghetti with crab meat, the spicy lobster, or the mussels with saffron.

€€€ Il Grottino, *Via del Mare 14, Santa Teresa di Gallura, T0789-754232. Easter-Sep daily 1200-1530 and 1900-2330, Oct-Easter Fri-Wed 1200-1530 and 1900-2330.* This small restaurant tucked down towards Rena Bianca has been growing in popularity for the past few years. Choose from fresh fish, meat or delicious pizza from a wood-burning oven. The mussel soup and grilled lamb are both good choices.

Cafés and bars
Caffè Conti, *Piazza Vittorio Emanuele I, Santa Teresa di Gallura, T0789-754271. Thu-Tue 0800-0230.* Cosy wooden interior with cool outdoor seating that's great for people-watching. Happy hour (1900-2100) has yummy freebies.

Mediterraneo Caffè, *Via Amsicora 7, Santa Teresa di Gallura, T0789-759014. Daily 0730-0230.* Two art deco-styled floors house the largest bar in town. In the summer, the open-air veranda is a welcome respite from the heat.

Interior Gallura *p36*
€€€ Il Purgatorio, *Via Garibaldi 9, Tempio Pausania, T079-634042. Wed-Mon 1900-2230.* A relative newcomer to Tempio, this restaurant is run by the town's well-respected *pasticceria* owner, Francesca Suelzu. Inside, wooden floors and granite walls add a touch of class to the delicious servings of mushrooms, *bottarga* and boar prosciutto served with pecorino cheese (by advance request).

€€ Bisson, *Via San Luca 18, Tempio Pausania, T079-632876.* Mon-Sat 2000-2300. Chef Pina Bisson tends to change her menu by the week, but usually carries sausage-based antipasti, ravioli with ricotta and a hint of lemon, and calamari. The restaurant also has a good selection of local wines from the Cantina Sociale di Tempio.

🎭 Entertainment

Olbia and around *p25*
Cinema
Cinema Olbia, *Via delle Terme 2, Olbia, T0789-82773.* Two screens with evening shows, right off the town's main drag.

Clubs
Capricorno Club, *Via Catello Piro 2, T0789-24700.* Tue-Thu 2100-0100, Fri-Sun 2100-0400. Central Olbia's only happening nightspot is this disco/bar, which plays anything from house to pop. Good cocktail selection.

South of Olbia *p26*
Clubs
Bal Harbour, *Via Stintino, San Teodoro, T0784-851052.* May-Sep Fri-Sun 2000-0400. This fashionable beachside restaurant and bar heats up at night when a swarm of well-dressed hipsters descends on its outdoor pool.
Jamila, *Via del Tirreno, San Teodoro, T339-251 2549.* May-Sep Fri-Sun 2200-0400. San Teodoro's most central disco is one of its most popular. Plop down on comfy red beds or dance the night away in this Arab-looking fantasy world.

Costa Smeralda and around *p27*
Children
Aquadream, *Località Baia Sardinia, T0789-99511.* Mid June-mid Sep daily 1030-1900, €18, €12 children. Never mind the pamphlet showing a woman in a thong being hosed down, this water park is actually geared towards children and has plenty of slides,

pools and games to keep the kiddies busy for a day.

Clubs
Billionaire, *Località Alto Pevero, T0789-94192.* Jun-Sep daily 0000-0500. As decadent as the name suggests, this is Costa Smeralda's plushest club. €30 gets you in with a drink… if the bouncers think you have what it takes. Splurge on a Methuselah of Cristal champagne for €35,000.
Phi Beach, *Località Baia Sardinia, T320-488 5180.* Jun-Sep daily noon-0300. An outdoor lounge with free music and dancing… although a Coke costs €10.
Sopravento, *Località Abbiadori, T0789-94717.* Jun-Sep daily 2300-0500. More of a rave-style club than Billionaire, with a mixed crowd.
Sottovento, *Località Abbiadori, T0789-92443.* Jun-Sep daily 2300-0500. Across the street from Sopravento, this older, more famous disco has a more intimate and typically Italian vibe.

✹ Festivals and events

Olbia and around *p25*
During July and August, Olbia hosts **L'Estate Olbiense**, with concerts and films in piazza Margherita.

South of Olbia *p26*
Isola Tavolara hosts a week-long film festival (cinematavolara.it) in mid to late July, at which Italian-language films are projected onto a giant outdoor screen by the beach.

Costa Smeralda and around *p27*
The Offshore Grand Prix is an annual sailing competition based in Porto Cervo in April.

Each June, racing cars descend on Porto Cervo's sandy paths for a leg of the **Italian Rally Championship**.

Parco Nazionale dell'Arcipelago di La Maddalena *p33*
On 22 July La Maddalena's residents parade through the streets to celebrate their patron saint, followed by music and plenty of food for all.

Interior Gallura *p36*
The character 'Giorgio', who represents a different political leader each year, is honoured as the king of Tempio Pausania during **Carnival** (31 Jan-5 Feb). He is burned on Shrove Tuesday to make way for the new king the following year. On **Good Friday**, the town's confraternity members don hoods and parade the streets carrying massive crucifixes. At the end of July, Tempio hosts international folk groups for the annual **Festa Internazionale del Folklore**.

⊙ Shopping

Costa Smeralda and around *p27*
There's plenty of high-end shopping to do in and around the Costa Smeralda. Your best bet is along **Porto Cervo**'s pedestrian *Passeggiata*.

Arzachena and around *p30*
Clothing and accessories
In Gyru, *Via Caprera 18, San Pantaleo, T338-432 2944. May-Oct daily 0930-1300 and 1700-2330*. Sells handmade women's dresses, sarongs and jewellery.

Northwest coast *p34*
Clothing and accessories
La Corallina, *Via XX Settembre 4, Santa Teresa di Gallura, T0789-754364. May-mid Oct daily 0930-1300 and 1600-2000*. This place has the best selection of jewellery made from the local coral that is gathered offshore.

Food and drink
La Bottega, *Via XX Settembre 5, Santa Teresa di Gallura, T0789-754216. May-mid Oct*

daily 0830-1300 and 1430-2300. Displays products from throughout the island: tuna from Carloforte, *bottarga* from Cabras, plus typical wine, cheese and spices.

Interior Gallura *p36*
For hand-woven rugs, visit **Aggius** (see page 36).

Clothing and accessories
Atelier Anna Grindi, *Via Roma 34-36, Tempio Pausania, T079-631864. Mon-Sat 0900-1200 and 1630-2000*. This imaginative designer makes dresses entirely from cork! Outfits range from €800 to €1600 and are fully washable. Also cork belts, travel bags and jewellery.

Food and drink
Pasticceria Luigi Carta, *Piazza Italia 1, Tempio Pausania, T079-632974. Mon 0900-1230, Tue-Sun 0900-1230 and 1630-2030*. A mouth-watering assortment of handmade cakes, cookies and gelato await you in this culinary tribute to Sardinian sweets.

Souvenirs
Arte Sughero di Sandra Cossu, *Via Tempio 19, Calangianus, T079-660505. Mon-Sat 0900-1300 and 1600-2000*. A collection of trays, jars, moulded *nuraghi* and other creative designs made from cork.

⊙ What to do

The Gallura *p23*
Boat trips
Chartered excursions from Palau around La Maddalena archipelago cost €35 with lunch included but they're packed with over 100 people aboard. For more breathing room, consider paying a bit more and hopping on the **Rumbera** (Porto di Palau, T348-006 2569, rumberacharter.com), a 13-m yacht that caters for a maximum of 14 people (€70-85 per person). Lunch and wine are served on board and frequent stops allow you to swim around the island's beaches.

Santa Teresa also offers numerous cruises around the archipelago and to Corsica; for details, visit the two tour companies at the corner of piazza Vittorio Emanuele I and via XX Settembre.

Diving
Porto San Paolo Diving Center, *Via Nenni 14, Porto San Paolo, T0789-40414, portospaolodiving.it*. This is the best of the town's numerous scuba outfits. Most dive trips visit the waters between Tavolara and Molara. Classes are available and gear can be rented. Non-certified divers can rent snorkel gear for just €15.

Horse riding
Sardigna Equitours, *Località Schifoni, San Teodoro, T329-414 8015, sardignaequitors.it*. Located between San Teodoro and Budoni, this stable organizes excursions into the mountains west of San Teodoro for views of the offshore islands and coast.

Watersports
Sporting Club Sardinia, *Località Porto Pollo, T0789-704016, portopollo.it. Mid Mar- mid Sep only*. This all-inclusive outfitter is your best bet of the three on the isthmus, offering diving, sailing, kitesurfing and windsurfing classes, plus laid-back boat excursions. The group also rents out bikes and mopeds and holds yoga classes. The California-style beach bar comes alive at night for music and dancing.

Well-being
Hotel Baja, *Via Nazionale, Cannigione, T0789-892041, hotelbaja.it*. Choose from full-body, hand and foot massages (€20- 130), to mud baths (€12-60) and beauty facials (€40-70).

⊖ Transport

The Gallura *p23*
From Olbia ARST runs frequent daily buses along the coast, including to San Teodoro

(40 mins) and Arzachena (35 mins). From Arzachena, buses continue to Porto Cervo (30 mins) and Baia Sardinia (40 mins). There are several daily buses from Olbia to Santa Teresa (1 hr 50 mins) and Tempio-Pausania (1 hr 20 mins) and a morning (0615) bus from Olbia to Sassari (1 hr 35 mins).

Trains connect Olbia with Cagliari (4 hrs) and Sassari (1 hr 50 mins). From June to September, the Trenino Verde tourist line runs twice daily between Tempio and Sassari (2 hrs 30 mins).

There are ferries from Olbia to Civitavecchia (8 hrs), Livorno (10 hrs) and Genoa (11 hrs), and from Golfo Aranci to Fiumicino (4 hrs 30 mins), Civitavecchia (7 hrs) and Livorno (6 hrs). Four to ten ferries leave Santa Teresa daily for Bonifacio, Corsica (55 mins).

Olbia *p25*
Olbia is small enough that you won't need a car. Buses 2 and 10 run from the airport to corso Umberto every 30 minutes from 0730 to 2000. ARST buses serve destinations along the coast and inland.

Bus station: **Stazione ARST**, corso Umberto 1, T0789-553000, arst.sardegna.it.

Train station: **Stazione Ferroviaria**, via Giacomo Pala, T0789-21197.

Parco Nazionale dell'Arcipelago di La Maddalena *p33*
Ferries, operated by **Delcomar** (T0781- 857123), **Enermar** (T0789-708484) and **Saremar** (T0789-727162), run from Palau to La Maddalena roughly three times every hour and take 20 minutes. A return trip costs €10-12 for foot passengers or €25-30 for a vehicle including passengers. On La Maddalena, buses leave from the intersection of piazza XXIII Febbraio and via Giovanni Amendola nine times a day and take the Panoramica route, stopping at each of the island's beaches; others continue to Caprera (13 times a day). Boat trips to the other islands depart from Cannigione, Palau, La Maddalena and Santa Teresa di Gallura.

ⓘ Directory

The Gallura *p23*

Money ATM at **Banca di Sassari**, corso Umberto 7, T0789-22371 (Mon-Sat 0830-1300 and 1445-1600). **Medical services Ospedale Civile**, via Aldo Moro, T0789-552200, 5 km north of town.

Farmacia Lupacciolu, Corso Umberto 134, T0789-202461 (Mon-Sat 0900-1300 and 1630-1930). **Post office Poste Italiane**, via Acquedotto, T0789-207400 (Mon-Fri 0800-1300, Sat 0800-1315). **Tourist information** There is a tourist booth on piazza Matteotti (Mon-Sat 0900-1400 and 1700-2000).

Contents

Sassari & the northwest

Northwest Sardinia offers so much rich evidence of its medieval past that much of it feels more Italian than Sardinian. More than anywhere else in Sardinia, the province of Sassari benefited from the bitter tug-of-war for power between rivals Genoa and Pisa. In addition to its provincial capital, Sassari, the Genoese gave the northwest two of the island's most attractive medieval towns: Castelsardo and Alghero, although the latter is renowned for having retained the distinctive Catalan spice and language it would learn from its later Aragonese rulers. For their part, the Pisans left a series of dazzling Romanesque churches in the Logudoro and Anglona regions, a reminder of the influence of Sardinia's independent *giudicati*.

There's ample evidence around Ozieri to suggest that the northwest corner was the earliest Sardinians' favourite part of the island. Their Bronze Age descendants built their finest work at Santu Antine and enough basalt towers around Torralba to warrant the name 'Valley of the nuraghi'. Elsewhere, you may find yourself scratching your head at the truncated pyramid of Monte d'Accodi, admiring the coastline of La Pelosa, and gripping your seat as you drive along nature's rollercoaster between Alghero and Bosa.

Home to 130,000 people, Sassari is the provincial capital and Sardinia's largest city after Cagliari, a fact that has created a certain rivalry between the two drastically different towns. While Cagliari basks in a soft beachside breeze, Sassari retains an inland air of legislative formality that has lingered from its proud past as a centre of political action.

Like Oristano, Sassari rose to prominence when pirate raids and disease forced residents of *Turris Libisonis* (modern-day Porto Torres) to retreat inland. By 1294, Sassari (then known as *Thathari*) was a power base from which Genoa could control commerce and expand its influence. However, unlike elsewhere in Sardinia, Sassari enjoyed legislative independence as a free commune, governed by a *Consiglio di Anziani* (group of elders). The *Sassaresi* soon outgrew their Genoese overlords and turned to Aragon in 1323 to help them rid the city of the Ligurians. The proud *Sassaresi* were not about to relinquish their autonomy, however, and rose up against the Aragonese in several rebellions before being finally subdued in 1420. Jesuits founded Sardinia's first university in Sassari in 1558 but a 17th-century malaria outbreak decimated half the population, creating widespread discontent that lingered long after. Only in the 19th century, when Sassari was connected to the SS131 highway, did it awaken again from its economic and cultural lull. During the First World War, the courageous Brigata Sassari regiment did much to rekindle Sassari's political fire, and the city produced two Italian presidents (Antonio Segni and Francesco Cossiga) as well as Communist leader Enrico Berlinguer in the 20th century.

Today, urban sprawl has surrounded Sassari's alluring, if crumbling, medieval quarter, but below its surface, the city remains the heart of Sardinia's political consciousness.

Museo Nazionale GA Sanna

ⓘ *Via Roma 64, T079-272203. Tue-Sun 0900-2000. €2, €1 concessions, free children and over-65s.*

Inside this neoclassical garden villa is Sardinia's most important historical museum after Cagliari's Museo Archeologico. The museum's two floors present a chronological history of Sardinia, from its Neolithic origins to the Roman conquest. The first room holds statues of the chubby mother goddess, obsidian arrowheads and a *domus de janas* grave with carved bull's head from Sardinia's Ozieri culture (3500-2700 BC). In the adjacent room, a display is dedicated to the Monte d'Accodi sanctuary (see page 56), with illustrations showing its rise from a Neolithic village to a raised temple. Menhirs feature prominently in the back room, many with carved daggers and trident-shaped human figures etched in their stone surfaces. Note the punctured skull in glass case No 18, demonstrating Neolithic and Copper Age surgery techniques used to 'release' the patient's illness.

Upstairs there are plastic recreations of nuraghi, sacred wells and *tombe di gigante* graves characteristic of Sardinia's Bronze Age. Most interesting are the mysterious *bronzetti* figurines, which raise one palm in peace while carrying a dagger in the other hand. Back downstairs, the museum concludes with Punic and Roman artefacts, such as tophet steles, necklaces and mosaic tiles.

Via Roma to Piazza Italia

Most of Sassari's social life takes place along via Roma, an attractive palm-lined avenue of cafés and bars. Across the street from the Sanna museum are the city's prison and courthouse. Via Roma concludes at Sassari's enormous centrepiece, the 18th-century

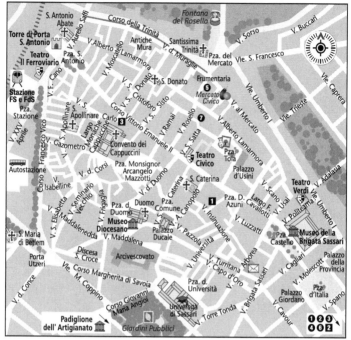

Where to stay 🛏

1 Casa Chiara
2 Frank Hotel
3 Vittorio Emanuele

Restaurants 🍴

1 Caffè Roma
2 Il Cenacolo
3 L'Antica Hostaria
4 Mocambo Café
5 Pizzeria Cocco
6 Trattoria Da Antonio
7 Trattoria L'Assassino

piazza Italia, presided over by a statue of Vittorio Emanuele II. The regal **Palazzo della Provincia** houses the local government and makes Cagliari's Palazzo Regio look provincially pedestrian by comparison. Inside, the bi-level **Sala Consiliari** ① *Mon-Thu 0815-1330 and 1600-1800*, has impressive frescoes of historical events in Sassari and pillars of the blinded Moor slaves depicted on Sardinia's flag.

Piazza Castello

To the northwest, piazza Castello symbolizes the city's history of foreign exploitation. Most noticeable are the two towering eyesores built by Fascist architects from the mainland in the 1940s (known tongue-in-cheek as Sassari's 'skyscrapers'). More significant, however, was the castle, built here by the Aragonese in 1330 and used as a Court of Inquisition. Its brutal torture regime included the decapitation of non-Catholics, the rape of young girls and the hanging of blonde men and women, who were once believed to represent the devil, upside down until blood gushed from their mouths. Animosity lingered long after the Spanish packed their bags and, in 1877, the *Sassaresi* demolished the structure. In late 2008, the square was being excavated in order to lay a glass walkway above the castle's ruins below.

A more positive chapter of Sardinian history can be found inside a working military barracks on the piazza. The modest **Museo Storico della Brigata Sassari** ① *piazza Castello 9, T079-208 5308, Mon-Thu 0800-1630, Fri-Sat 0800-1200, free*, is dedicated to the decorated Brigata Sassari regiment that fought valiantly in the First World War and displays sandbag trenches, helmets, rifles, photographs from the front and letters from international officers commending the Brigata's courage.

Corso Vittorio Emanuele

From piazza Castello, corso Vittorio Emanuele shoots west into Sassari's oldest and most appealing neighbourhood: its medieval district. The *corso* was part of the ancient Roman road connecting Cagliari and Porto Torres and later became the prime address for Sassari's medieval elite. Today, it is one of Sassari's main shopping thoroughfares, with modern boutiques interspersed between medieval Aragonese buildings. For many years, Sassari's once proud *centro storico* was in a state of neglect and its Gothic *palazzi* were falling into disrepair. However, serious restoration is now underway and it's not uncommon to see entire streets uprooted and awaiting repair, forcing pedestrians to use wooden beams to cross the street.

The 15th-century **Casa Farris** at No 23 certainly shows its age, retaining (if barely) two Catalan-Gothic double windows. Much better preserved is the Casa di Re Enzo at No 42, in the same style and from the same period. It houses a clothing store but you can step inside its portico to admire the sculptured capitals and ceiling frescoes. The bottom of the corso is marked by the di Sant'Antonio column, engraved with historical scenes from Sassari by Sassarese Eugenio Tavolara in 1954.

Teatro Civico

① *Corso Vittorio Emanuele 35, T331-4377156. Museum Mon-Fri 1600-2100, with guided visits in English (call ahead). Free.*

Restored in 2006 and reopened in 2008, Sassari's civic theatre holds the city's tourist office as well as a first-rate museum of *Sassarese* culture. The neoclassical theatre was built between 1826 and 1829 above the 13th-century Palazzo di Città where Sassari's *Consiglio di Anziani* held court in the 13th and 14th centuries.

Inside, the museum wraps around the theatre's ballroom on three levels, allowing visitors a backstage pass to its stage and seating and providing computer touch-screen graphics that detail the city's sights with videos (in Italian). Upstairs, you can look down on the corso from a wrought iron balcony, just as Sassari's mayor does on the day of the *Candaleri* (see page 71). If you can't make it for the real thing or for Sassari's Holy Week, the museum has videos of both events as well as small-scale statues depicting the festivities' various participants. The tour concludes with a display of peasant costumes worn in 19th-century Sassari, revealing a decidedly Spanish influence.

Duomo di San Nicola

① *Piazza Duomo, T079-232067. Daily 0900-1200 and 1600-1900, free.*

In the middle of Sassari's narrow beehive of medieval streets, the magnificent Baroque façade of the San Nicola cathedral stands head and shoulders above its surroundings. The towering 18th-century front shows the Giudicato of Torres' coat of arms and the three martyred saints, Gavino, Proto and Gianuario (see page 55). A statue of San Nicola presides over the saints, while God the Father blesses the cathedral from its highest point. The façade was tacked on to the 15th-century Catalan-Gothic church, which in turn was built over a 13th-century Romanesque original. Today, only parts of the campanile and the façade's base survive from the 13th century.

The Gothic interior is not nearly as flashy as the exterior but it does contain some impressive pieces. The second chapel on the right has a 17th-century canvas of the Virgin dedicated to saints Cosma and Damiano, while, beside the altar, another 17th-century canvas shows San Elgio with scenes of Sassari. The cathedral's small **Museo del Tesoro** in the sacristy holds the fine 14th-century *Madonna del Bosco* painting, as well as a silver statue of San Gavino.

Chiesa di Santa Maria di Betlem
ⓘ *Piazza di Santa Maria, T079-235740. Daily 0800-1200 and 1600-1930, free.*
Built by Benedictine monks in 1106 and enlarged by Franciscans in the 13th century, this church actually predates the city around it. A series of heavy restorations from the 16th to 19th centuries has greatly altered the church's appearance, so that the lower part of the façade is all that remains of the original 12th-century structure. A 15th-century rose window highlights the Gothic façade's capitals and columns, though the Catalan architects also showed hints of Islamic influences in the large dome and slender campanile.

Inside, the church has fallen victim to some clumsy Baroque facelifts but it preserves its 15th-century plan of cross-vaulted Gothic chapels lining the church's single nave. Each chapel is dedicated to one of Sassari's craft guilds, which parade during the *Li Candaleri* procession; the most impressive is the bricklayers' *Cappella dei Muratori* to the left of the entrance.

Sassari's fortifications
By the mid 14th century, Sassari was surrounded by a moat, defensive walls and 36 towers, which gave their name to the region's independent authority, the Giudicato of Torres. The fortifications had largely fallen down by the 19th century when city planners toppled them, but a few remnants still survive. **Piazza Sant'Antonio** holds the last remaining tower with full battlements, while **corso Trinità** preserves the largest stretch of Sassari's walls, complete with *Thathari's* coat of arms. At the eastern end of corso Trinità is **Porta Rosello**, the only surviving medieval gate of the four that allowed entrance through the walls.

Fontana di Rosello
ⓘ *Opposite Porta Rosello. Park May-Sep Tue-Sat 0900-1300 and 1730-2030, Sun 1730-2030, Oct-Apr Tue-Sat 0900-1300 and 1600-1900, Sun 0900-1300, free.*
In a park opposite the Porta Rosello is this white marble fountain, built by the Genoese in 1295 over a natural spring. Makeovers in 1606 and 1828 gave the structure its present shape, with four statues at the fountain's corners representing the seasons and open-mouthed lions shooting water into a basin. The fountain is capped by two arches and a statue of San Gavino riding a horse – all of which bares an uncanny resemblance to a shopping bag. Fittingly in a politically charged city, those unhappy with Sassari's government in the past have unearthed the surrounding cobblestones and pelted the fountain with them, which perhaps explains the structure's frequent restorations.

Porto Torres and around → *For listings, see pages 66-74.*

On the coast north of Sassari, Porto Torres is littered with petrochemical refineries that spoil first impressions of the island when approached from the sea. However, the area boasts two of Sardinia's archaeological gems, spread ten minutes and nearly 4000 years apart: the island's finest Romanesque church and a mysterious truncated pyramid predating those in Egypt.

Porto Torres was founded by Julius Caesar in 46 BC as *Turris Libisonis*, after his victory in a battle in Libya, and remained a key port well into the Middle Ages when it was the capital of the Giudicato of Torres. The pirate raids and malaria that ravaged coastal Sardinia under Aragonese and Spanish rule hit hard here, and the port waned until the Savoyards relaid the ancient Roman road from Cagliari to Porto Torres, pumping new life and industry into the town.

Basilica Romanica di San Gavino

① *Porto Torres, T347-400 1288. Mon-Sat 0900-1300 and 1500-1800, Sun 1100-1300 and 1500-1900. Free, €1.50 to visit the crypt.*

Signs at the top of corso Vittorio Emanuele point towards the oldest and largest Romanesque church in Sardinia, the Basilica di San Gavino. It's a real diamond in the suburban rough, an imposing limestone structure finished in 1080 by the Pisans which, oddly enough, has two rounded apses at its ends instead of a façade. The basilica owes its name to a Roman soldier, Gavino, who was charged with watching over two priests, Proto and Gianuario, who had been sent by the Pope to Christianize the Sardinians but were jailed by the Romans. After witnessing their faith, Gavino released the two prisoners and converted to Christianity. The three were soon captured, decapitated in 304, and have remained the subject of religious rapture in Sardinia ever since.

Inside the limestone exterior, the basilica's central nave is flanked by 11 marble columns on each side taken from the Roman settlement nearby. Small windows let faint light slip through, illuminating a few frescoes and statues in a hauntingly dim glow. A staircase leads to a 17th-century crypt containing five statues in Carrara marble and the urns of the three martyrs resting in Roman sarcophagi.

Antiquarium

① *Via Ponte Romano 99, T0795-14433, ibiscoop.com. Tue-Sun 0900-2000, €2, €1 concessions.*

Dwarfed by an octagonal Aragonese watchtower directly behind it, the Roman column at the intersection of corso Vittorio Emanuele and the Lungomare marks the official end of the Romans' Karalibus–Turrem highway (the modern-day SS131). To the left by the railway station is the Antiquarium archaeological museum and an excavated area, showing what remains of the Roman port of Turris Libisonis. In spring, 2009 the archaeological site was still closed for repairs with no plans to re-open anytime soon but, peering through the museum window, you can make out rows of *insulae* flats, columns, streets and a massive thermal spa that had hot, cold and tepid baths. The thermal monument is known as the **Palazzo di Re Barbaro** (Barbarian King's Palace) because, before archaeologists got their hands on it, Porto Torres' citizens had thought the structure was the fortress of the king who martyred the town's three saints.

The museum displays artefacts from the site and has an excellent second-floor model of the Roman settlement. Highlights include an altar dedicated to the Egyptian god Bubastis from AD 35 and some well-preserved mosaic tiles.

East of Porto Torres

The *Sassaresi* have adopted nearby **Platamona** as their city beach. By Sardinian standards it's nothing special but it's a perfectly pleasant and lively place, capped by a crumbling

Aragonese tower. A wooden walkway runs along the bird-friendly **Stagno di Platamona** marsh. The road east cuts through more pines and sand dunes until you reach **Marina di Sorso**, reputed to be a great surf-casting spot. Inland, **Sorso** is known for its Cannonau wine.

Monte D'Accodi

ⓘ *Km 222, SS131 (only accessible from the south-bound carriageway) between Porto Torres and Sassari, T334-807 4449. Late Jun-Sep Mon-Sat 1000-2000, Oct and late Feb-late Jun Mon-Sat 0900-1900, Nov-late Feb Mon-Sat 0900-1400, free.*

This often overlooked structure is one of the most intriguing ancient sites in Sardinia. In the middle of a pasture sits a truncated pyramid temple built with limestone rocks rising to 11 m that perfectly resembles a Mesopotamian ziggurat (a terraced altar from ancient Babylon). Dating from 2800 BC (nearly 200 years before the oldest Egyptian pyramid) and attributed to the Ozieri Culture, it's the world's only example of such a Copper Age structure outside Babylonia (modern-day Iraq). How and why Sardinia's indigenous population built such a structure remains unknown. During the Second World War, the Nazis used the holy shrine's elevated terrace as a cannon launching pad to shoot down aeroplanes!

The temple, which was destroyed by a fire and rebuilt in 2600 BC, consists of a long ramp rising to meet the three-tiered sanctuary whose 30 m by 38 m rectangular apex aligns perfectly with the cardinal points and was once crowned by a shrine. Inside the temple, a statue of the pre-Nuraghic chubby mother goddess was found inside a single room painted in red ochre.

To the left and right of the ramp, respectively, are a large menhir and two sacrificial altars dating from between 4500 and 4300 BC. You can still see the holes punched through the tops of the altars to secure animals for sacrificial slaughter. By the larger altar, there are two perfectly smooth, circular *omphalos* (navels of the world) stones commonly used in ancient Greece – on which shells were placed as votive offerings.

The Logudoro → *For listings, see pages 66-74.*

The area southeast of Sassari is a relatively flat expanse of farmland whose vast grain fields have given it the name Logudoro ('golden place'). The few communities sprinkled throughout this area preserve the purest form of Sardo around, the mellifluous Logudorese. Bronze Age nuraghi builders left their highest concentration of towers around Torralba, and also their most spectacular monument at Santu Antine. In the Middle Ages, the Logudoro thrived under the Giudicato of Torres and reminders of its splendour are visible in a string of Romanesque churches rivalling anything on the Italian mainland.

Ozieri

Built in a natural amphitheatre between two hills, Ozieri was the home of Sardinia's most celebrated prehistoric civilization, the so-called Ozieri Culture (3500-2700 BC. Many artefacts from these Neolithic people have been retrieved from the **Grotte di San Michele** ⓘ *vicolo San Michele, T329-266 9436, Tue-Sat 0900-1300 and 1500-1800, Sun-Mon 0930-1230, €3.50, €2.50 children or €5/4 including museum*, near the top of town, and are on display, alongside relics from the subsequent Nuraghic to Byzantine periods, at the **Museo Archeologico** ⓘ *piazza San Francesco, T079-785 1052, Tue-Sat 0900-1300 and 1600-1900, Sun 0930-1230, €4, €3 children or €5, €4 children including cave*.

Modern Ozieri is set on a slope leading from the bus depot at piazza Garibaldi to its main square, **piazza Carlo Alberto**, where tall 18th-century houses retain their *suttea* (verandas), lined with Doric columns. From the piazza, via Vittorio Emanuele III ascends to the 12th-century marble **Fontana Grixoni**, named after the *Ozierese* who funded it. In nearby piazza Duomo is the neoclassical **Cattedrale dell'Immacolata**, whose campanile stands tall, topped by a multi-coloured dome. Inside, there's a famous 16th-century retable by the 'Maestro di Ozieri'.

Nuraghe Santu Antine and Valle dei Nuraghi
ⓘ *Off the SS131 at km 172, south of Torralba, T079-847298, nuraghesantuantine.it. Daily 0900-sunset, €3 including Torralba museum, €2 children.*
The town of Torralba is surrounded by 32 nuraghi and numerous *tombe di giganti*, making it the centre of the densest concentration of Nuraghic sites in Sardinia and earning it the title, 'Valle dei Nuraghi'. But if you only see one of Sardinia's more than 7000 Bronze Age towers, it should be Nuraghe Santu Antine, the crowning opus of this mysterious culture.

The site is surrounded by 10 circular Nuraghic-age huts and six rectangular huts made by the Romans who dismantled parts of the original structure to make stables. A lintel opening leads to a large courtyard with a well from where you can admire the masterpiece of this Bronze Age settlement: a three-storey central keep rising 17.5 m and joined to three surrounding towers enclosed by a triangular-shaped wall. The whole structure was built in the 16th century BC. The keep preserves its *tholos* dome roof and, below, three niches lead to an encircling tunnel connecting it to the surrounding towers.

In the courtyard, two flights of steps and a staircase ascend to the first floor. Here, the ground floor's tunnel-chamber pattern is repeated on a slightly smaller scale. The spiral staircase continues to the second floor where the base and lip of the *tholos* dome remain, but its walls have collapsed, turning it into a terrace. In its heyday, the fortress rose to 25 m; you can make out traces of the stairwell winding up to a terrace on the third level, from where several other of Torralba's nuraghi are visible. The Santu Antine ticket gets you in to the town's **Museo della Valle dei Nuraghi** ⓘ *via Carlo Felice 143, T079-847296, daily 0900-sunset*, which has artefacts and pictures from Torralba's many nuraghi and *tombe di giganti*.

Necropoli di Sant'Andrea di Priu
ⓘ *10 km east of Bonorva, T079-867894. Jun-Sep Tue-Sun 1000-1300 and 1500-1900, or by appointment, €2.*
Ten kilometres south of Torralba on the SS131 is the town of Bonorva, built on a plateau. Follow signs from here towards Bono to reach the Neolithic Necropoli di Sant'Andrea di Priu. Situated at the end of a dirt road, the site preserves 18 *domus de janas* tombs excavated by the Ozieri Culture from the volcanic rock. The highlight is the **Tomba del Capo**, which was reused as a Christian cult in the Middle Ages. Some of the area's archaeological finds can be seen at Bonorva's **Museo Archeologico** ⓘ *piazza Sant'Antonio, T079-867894, Jun-Sep Tue-Sun 1000-1300 and 1500-1900, or by appointment, €2 or €4 with Sant'Andrea di Priu.*

A tour of Logudoro's Romanesque churches
During the Middle Ages, Sardinia's autonomous *giudicati* hired Pisan merchants and religious orders to work alongside local artists in the construction of churches. The result is a series of Romanesque masterpieces that now lies abandoned in fields, adding to their mystique.

Many of the churches are conveniently clustered along the SS597 making for a great day trip from Sassari if you have your own wheels. The tour lasts several hours, and it's hard to digest history on an empty stomach, so pick up supplies at Sassari's Antica Salumeria Mangatia (see page 72) before you head out; you'll need them later.

The tour starts, high up, 15 km southeast of Sassari on the SS597, at the **Chiesa della Santissima Trinità di Saccargia** ① *T347-000 7882, Apr-Oct daily 0900-1900, by reservation only at other times, €2.* Horizontal bands of white limestone and black basalt cover the building like zebra stripes. The church was consecrated in 1116 by the *giudice* of Torres to thank the Virgin of Saccargia for helping his wife conceive, and is allegedly named after a 'dappled cow' (*sa acca argia* in Sardo) that would kneel in prayer at the site; look for four carved cows on the front capital. Inside, the church is built on a T-shaped cross with a single nave and transept. Thirteenth-century frescoes adorn the central apse with scenes from the Old and New Testaments. Three kilometres east, there's no sign for the abandoned **San Michele di Salvènero**, but you'll see it on your right after the 4-km marker. Take the gravel road from the SS597 to get a closer look.

Ten kilometres further, follow signs to Ardara and **Santa Maria del Regno** ① *T079-400193, daily 0800-1200 and 1600-1900, free.* The 12th-century church and its squat bell tower face south, presumably so that the sun can illuminate its deep red trachyte façade. Inside, paintings adorn each of the columns lining the central nave. The church is said to hold the remains of many *Logudorese* rulers, including its last *giudicessa*, Adelasia.

At Km 22 on the SS597, look for the left-hand turning to **Chiesa di Sant'Antonio di Bisarcio** ① *daily 0900-1300 and 1500-1900, €1.50,* perched on a bluff. Rebuilt between 1170 and 1190 after a fire destroyed the 11th-century original, it incorporates French influences, such as its atrium porch, into the Pisan-Romanesque design. Though a lightning bolt severed the church's campanile, the interior's three narrow naves are well preserved.

You may hit sheep traffic on the 20-km stretch east to **Nostra Signora di Castro** ① *daily 0900-1700,* on the shores of the Lago del Coghinas. The church is surrounded by *cumbessiàs* (dwellings for pilgrims), which are still used between 13th and 19th April each year, when Oschiri's faithful carry a statue of the Virgin to the site from their church. Hungry? Find a table near the church's car park, unwrap your picnic and enjoy the lakeside vista.

Alghero → *For listings, see pages 66-74.*

Suitably, Sardinia's most touristy town is also its most attractive. Colourful campaniles and sandstone palazzi preside over cobblestone streets inside its medieval walls, while the Mediterranean breaks against its seaside bastions on the west side. Yet, Alghero developed as a Catalan colony and is arguably the island's least 'Sardinian' town.

In the 12th century, the powerful Genoese Doria family wanted a foothold in Sardinia, so they transformed two tiny coastal villages – Castelgenovese (Castelsardo) and present-day Alghero – into fortified strongholds, naming the latter *Aleguerium* (algae). Aleguerium's strategic port attracted frequent raids. It was briefly taken over by Genoa's arch-rival, Pisa, in the 1280s and underwent 30 years of local riots before the Catalan-Aragonese eventually took control in 1353, renaming it *Alguer*. Rebellions continued until King Pere the Ceremonious sailed over a year later, expelled the unruly population to Sardinia's interior and repopulated his colony with obedient Iberians. Doria's ramparts came crumbling down and a taller, turreted wall sprang up as Alguer was named an official Aragonese royal city in 1501. The discovery of America led to the decline of Alguer's port and, even after the Savoyards took control in 1720, the population remained bound to Catalonia. The landward walls toppled in 1876 and, with its belt loosened, Alghero has since sprawled inland.

After nearly 400 years of Iberian rule, the *Algheresi* still doggedly maintain their Catalan heritage to such an extent that the town is referred to warmly by its Spanish cousins as 'Little Barcelona'. Street signs are written in both Italian ('*via*') and Catalan ('*carrer*') forms, Iberian-Gothic architecture abounds, recipes – such as the spicy *algherese* paella – mirror Spanish cuisine, and, most tellingly, an archaic form of Catalan is still spoken by old-timers and children alike.

Inside Alghero's walls

Alghero's medieval centre wears its age well. Beyond the arch of **Porta a Mare**, with its Aragonese coat of arms, the elegantly weathered **piazza Civica** gives a good first impression. The triangular square was home to Aragon's government and its most important families. Spanish Emperor Carlos V famously proclaimed, "You are all knights!" to the delight of the *Algheresi* from the second-storey window of the square's stately **Palazzo D'Albis** (No 32) in 1541.

Due west in piazza Duomo is Alghero's main religious landmark, the **Cattedrale di Santa Maria**, whose four oversized Doric columns nearly cover its façade. Like Cagliari's cathedral, Santa Maria is a medley of Renaissance, Baroque, and Gothic styles. The campanile and portal are from the original 1552 construction and modelled on the Gothic cathedral in Barcelona; they're best seen from via Principe Umberto behind the church. Nearby, the **Museo Diocesano d'Arte Sacra** ① *piazza Duomo, T079-975350, Sun-Tue 1000-1230, Thu-Fri 1030-1830, Sat 1000-1230 and 1600-1900, €4, €3 concessions*, sits inside the Chiesa del Rosario. The museum holds Spanish silverware, woodcarvings and a marble statue of the Madonna della Miseracordia. However, the most interesting display is the collection of stamped lithographs of Sardinian Romanesque churches.

Four-storey Catalan-Gothic buildings hold their breath along the claustrophobically tight **via Carlo Alberto** and **via Roma**, Alghero's main shopping arteries and site of the evening *passeggiata*. Beyond the sea of shop windows selling Alghero's blood-red coral jewellery, look for the 15th-century **Chiesa di San Francesco**. The church's original Gothic façade was redone in 1598 in Catalan Renaissance-Romanesque style, complete with two rose windows. The church's sandstone pillars, chapels and belltower are original and take centre stage for Alghero's Good Friday procession. Continue up via Carlo Alberto to the Baroque **Chiesa di San Michele** where a marble dove presides over the church's bare façade. Built by the Jesuits in 1589, the church is best known for its colourful majolica dome that dominates Alghero's skyline.

Along Alghero's walls

There were two main entrances to the Genoese medieval town. Alghero's wealthy Jewish community erected the **Torre di Porta Terra** land entrance in 1360, which was linked by a drawbridge to the Gothic arch now serving as a First World War memorial. Like in Cagliari's Castello district, the gate closed each day at dusk and any Sardinian caught inside was subject to a harsh penalty. (The tower now serves as a tourist information office). The seaside entrance was the **Porta a Mare** (see above).

When the Catalans refortified Alghero in the 1500s, they ringed their royal city with a commanding wall and seven towers, which still remain. You can see remnants of the enclosing wall at the **Torre di San Giovanni**. Towards the sea, the 22-m **Torre Sulis** is Alghero's tallest tower and was named after the Sardinian patriot, Vincenzo Sulis, who was convicted of treason in 1799 and imprisoned inside for 21 years. The tower marks the beginning of the town's seafront bastion, a parapet that grips the town like a strong

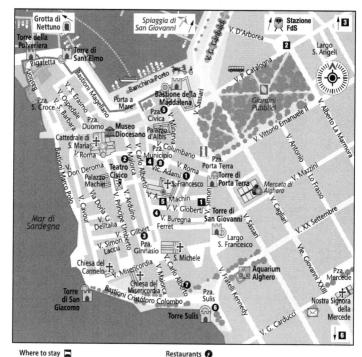

Where to stay 🛏

1 Aigua
2 Catalunya
3 La Mariposa
4 Mamajuana
5 San Francesco
6 Villa Las Tronas

Restaurants 🍴

1 Al Refettorio
2 Al Tugari
3 Birreria Sant Miquel
4 Café del Corso
5 Gelateria Arcobaleno
6 Il Pavone
7 La Lepanto
8 La Posada del Mar

arm to keep it from falling into the Mediterranean, and creates Sardinia's most romantic *Lungomare* promenade. Each section is named after an explorer.

Bastioni Cristoforo Colombo leads west to the **Torre di San Giacomo**, called the '*Torre dels Cutxos*' (dogs' tower) by the *Algheresi* because the octagonal structure was used as a kennel for strays for much of the 20th century. From here, Bastioni Marco Polo heads north to **La Garitta** tower, which sailors used as a primitive lighthouse by placing a lantern inside, while the 18th-century **Torre de la Polveriera**, behind, held gun powder and weapons.

A few steps away, the **Torre di Sant'Elmo** is dedicated to the saint of navigators. The final tower, the **Torre della Maddalena** overlooking the port, has the best preserved remnants of Alghero's original interior bastions and holds an outdoor theatre in its connecting rampart.

Outside Alghero's walls

Alghero's port offers daily boat trips from April to October to spot dolphins and tour Capo Caccia (see page 72). A cycling and jogging path shoots north from here towards the marina, from where you can hire boats, and to Alghero's city beach, **Spiaggia di San Giovanni**.

Across via Sassari from the Torre della Maddalena are the **Giardini Pubblici**, which have a large children's playground and makeshift carnival rides in warm months. Further south, the **Mare Nostrum Aquarium** ① *Via XX Settembre 1, T079-978333, Apr-Oct Sat 1500-2000, Sun 1000-1300 and 1500-2000. Oct-Apr hours vary, €8, €5 children*, holds sharks, piranhas and a few reptiles and amphibians.

Driving the Alghero–Bosa coastal road

One of Sardinia's most scenic coastal roads connects two of its most attractive medieval towns: Alghero and Bosa. For 42 km the Litoranea Panoramica offers spectacular views of the coast as it slaloms around volcanic cliffs, with the slick rock face on one side and the mountainous *macchia* on the other. This route can be undertaken as a leisurely drive or a full-day bike trip. However you travel, pack a bathing suit, look for hidden beaches behind the hairpin turns and bring your own supplies because there won't be any towns or houses in sight!

The first bathing spot, **Spiaggia La Speranza**, is 8 km south of Alghero. A bar/restaurant along its curling strand is your last chance to stock up on food or water before the 35-km stretch to Bosa. Watch for griffon vultures coasting on the *maestrale* winds as you twist south. Several watchtowers, and lots of goats, are visible as you descend around **Capo Marargiu**. Dirt paths often lead down to sheltered patches from the roadside parking spots; there's one 5 km north of Bosa near the Torre Argentina.

After spending the night in Bosa, serious cyclists who do not want to retrace the same route can take the SS292 inland road for 60 km back to Alghero, stopping at Padria, a hillside village with a **Museo Archeologico** ① *via Nazionale 1, T079-807018, May-Sep Tue-Sun 1600-1830, €1*, and at **Villanova Monteleone**, whose morning farmers' market is a great place to pick up supplies.

Around Alghero → *For listings, see pages 66-74.*

The coast west from Alghero to Capo Caccia is known as the Riviera del Corallo after the rare red corallium rubrum that grows in the coast's dark caves. Fishermen have collected the stuff for centuries and it remains big business for jewellers. Divers should spend time around the Riviera, especially in Nereo's Cave, the largest underwater cave in the Mediterranean (see page 73) and everyone should make the trip to one of Sardinia's must-see sights, the Grotta di Nettuno. Before you head west, however, check out two contrasting attractions, north of town.

Necropoli di Anghelu Ruju

① *10 km north of Alghero towards Porto Torres, T079-994 4394, coopsilt.it. Easter-Oct daily 0900-1800, Nov-Easter daily 1000-1400. €3 or €5 with Nuraghe Palmavera.*

Don't drive too fast after the turn-off for the airport 9 km north of Alghero or you'll miss the white, hand-written sign for one of the region's prime Neolithic attractions, Anghelu Ruju. The site preserves 37 *domus de janas* burial chambers, dug from sandstone by the Ozieri Culture between 3300 and 2900 BC and reused until 1500 BC by their successors. The earliest tombs were primitive caves, while the later ones appear as symmetrical T-shaped mass graves, where up to 30 men, women and children were buried, some partly cremated, others skinned beforehand.

Like ancient Egyptians, Sardinia's superstitious Nuraghic population designed these tombs to mirror the living quarters of those they eternally housed. Later tombs, such as those immediately to the right as you enter, had multiple rooms with carved beds, doorways and architraves. Many have geometric figures and bulls' heads engraved in the rock face: if you crouch down in Tomb 'A' you can make out six of these horned heads above the rectangular cut-out door. Bulls were regarded as a symbol of strength during this period, whose sacrificed blood had regenerative powers. Neolithic Sardinians carved bull heads on their tombs to represent the sacrifice of an individual's ancestors, believing it would spur fertility in the village, a practice still echoed in the Barbagie during Carnival (see page 80).

Sella and Mosca Cantina

ⓘ Località I Piani, T079-997700, sellaemosca.com. Tours Jun-Sep daily 1730 or by advanced booking. Enoteca Jun-Sep daily 0830-2030, Oct-May daily 0830-1830. Visitors should always call ahead to check opening times.

Six hundred metres up the road from the necropolis, you'll see the sign for Sardinia's most renowned wine producer, Sella & Mosca. Set on 650 hectares of vineyards, the winery produces nationally prized Torbato, Carignano, Vermintino and Cannonau wines, as well as Sardinia's esteemed *mirto* liquor and *filu e' ferru* grappa under the label Zedda Piras, all of which are for sale at the site's cantina.

The estate's lush gardens include its own church and a former school for the labourers' children. There's also a museum (summer only) displaying vintage photographs by Vittorio Sella of the company's early wine production. Another museum houses artefacts found at the Anghelu Ruju archaeological site, which was part of Sella & Mosca's property until they donated it to the *comune*.

Fertilia

Sandy beaches line the coast west of Alghero, connected by bike paths that nearly reach as far as Fertilia. The town ('Fertileville') was one of Mussolini's imaginatively named land reclamation schemes and was repopulated with farmers from Ferrara, who built the austere dark stone parish church and campanile. The place resembles an army barracks, with an arcaded main street that offers little relief from the otherwise right-angled austerity.

Just inland is Alghero's airport, while on the coast to the west are two prime beaches, **Le Bombarde** and **Lazzaretto**.

Nuraghe Palmavera

Less than a kilometre past Spiaggia Lazzaretto, the crumbling remains of Nuraghe Palmavera nearly tumble into the road. The village dates back to the 15th century BC and preserves two towers: the first in limestone and the second in sandstone surrounded by roughly 50 circular huts. Archaeologists insist that another 150 huts lie buried between the road and the sea and that, in the village's golden age around the ninth century BC, it housed 800 people. The reunion hut, where the elders held court and performed religious rituals, dates from this period. At its centre is a remarkable model of a nuraghe, leading some archaeologists to believe that the Bronze Age towers became the subject of cult worship by subsequent generations.

Porto Conte and Noah's Ark

The holiday community of Porto Conte is named after the calm, crescent-shaped bay that stretches from Punta Giglio in the east to Capo Caccia in the west. A flat road rings the bay, going north around pine and eucalyptus groves, and doubles as a wonderful jogging or cycling route. The area's two most popular beaches, **Mugoni** and **La Stalla** are signposted right next to each other.

On their way to Capo Caccia, nature lovers should stop off at the **Foresta Demaniale Le Prigionette** ⓘ *Km 5, SP55, T079-949060, Mon-Fri 0800-1600, Sat-Sun 0900-1700.* The site of a former prison, the park consists of 1,200 ha of protected land and is nicknamed *'L'arca di Noè'* (Noah's Ark) because of the diverse animals that have been introduced here since the 1970s, turning it into a virtual zoo of Sardinian fauna: deer from central Sardinia, miniature horses from the Giara plateau and albino donkeys from Asinara, among others. Two hiking trails criss-cross between ilex trees, heather and strawberry scrub and end at Cala della Barca with views of Isola Piana.

Capo Caccia and the Grotta di Nettuno

South of Porto Conte, the road climbs past the placid Tramariglio and Dragunara bays and their Aragonese towers to the 107-m peak of Capo Caccia. Turn right at the *'Panoramica'* sign to peer out over the windswept and barren **Isola Foradada** from the edge of Cala dell'Inferno (Hell's Cove). This is one of Sardinia's more dramatic and popular places to watch the sun set, so come early.

The road dead-ends at the ticket office for one of Europe's most renowned caves, the **Grotta di Nettuno** ⓘ *T079-946540, tours every hour, Apr-Sep daily 0800-1900, Oct daily 0900-1800, Nov-Mar daily 0900-2000, closed during rain or rough seas, €10, €5 children.* For the past 100 million years, nature has been hard at work battering Capo Caccia's limestone base with rough waves and constant winds to hollow out this spectacular 2.5-km cavern, and it makes visitors work hard too: to reach the cave's entrance you must either descend for 110 m down the steep 656-step Escala del Cabirol or arrive by boat from Alghero's port. The round-trip by boat takes about 2½ hrs and is operated by **Traghetti Navisarda** ⓘ *T079-978961, navisarda.it,* with departures hourly 0900-1700 from June to September, and at 0900, 1000 and 1500 only in April, May and October; purchase tickets (€12, €6 children) at the port.

Once inside the cave, the 200-m guided tour skirts the Lago Lamarmora, a saltwater lake fed by the sea and goes from the first chamber to the Smith Room, named after one of the cave's early explorers. Backlights allow you to marvel at a wonderland of stalactites, stalagmites and columns coloured from orange to a deep green, with nicknames like the 'Christmas Tree', 'Grand Organ' and 'Cupola'. The cavern shelters a small, sandy beach inside and saves its most delicate treasure for last: the Lace Room, where thousands of crystallized creations dangle from the ceiling like a stitched pattern.

The Nurra → *For listings, see pages 66-74.*

North of Capo Caccia, the landscape flattens out into a fertile valley covered by farmland and eucalyptus trees, forming Sardinia's northwestern corner, the Nurra. Along the way, signs indicate Lago Baratz, Sardinia's only natural lake, where pine trees and sand dunes keep what little water there is from escaping to the sea. The region's star attraction, however, is a beach of jaw-dropping beauty, La Pelosa. Beyond its shelving shoreline lies the uninhabited Asinara national park, home to the world's only breed of albino donkey.

Stintino

Where Sardinia's northwestern tip narrows to a sliver lies the sunny fishing community of Stintino. The village takes its name from the Sardo word *'isthintinu'* (narrow passage) and was founded in 1885, when 45 fishing families of Ligurian descent were displaced from their homes on Asinara island to make way for a state prison. Until 1972, the *Stintinesi* held an annual tuna *mattanza*, but the industrial boom in Porto Torres in the 1970s and '80s warmed the surrounding waters, changing the tuna's migration and effectively killing the industry. Like Carloforte (another Ligurian outpost), Stintino today is a medley of colourful, boxy houses on the water but the population hasn't kept up the traditional dialect or trade, and it's now tourists, not tuna, that drive the economy. Over 50,000 tourists descend on the area each summer to splash around Stintino's luminous beaches, so book ahead if you plan to come here in high season.

Stintino juts out from between two ports: the old Porto Minori for fishing boats and the newer Porto Mannu for yachts, where you can find information on excursions to Asinara. This is also where you'll find a trailer housing the **Museo della Tonnara** ① *Porto Mannu, T079-512209, May-Sep Tue-Sun 1800-2400, €1.55, €1 children*, which recalls the glory days of the tuna trade and is cleverly modelled on the fishermen's six-chambered tuna nets, finishing in the *camera della morte* (deathbed).

La Pelosa

Throughout Italy, Stintino is synonymous with beaches. The most magnificent is La Pelosa, which lies 3.5 km north at Capo Falcone. Anyone who's ever posted a letter in Italy might already be familiar with the scene, as La Pelosa is one of two images – along with the Tuscan countryside – that the Italian post features on its stamps to illustrate Italy's natural beauty. A spherical patch of flour-white sand slowly shelves into the turquoise sea, changing hue with the varying depths. From the beach, you can wade out to a small island housing the 16th-century **Torre Pelosa** just offshore or look out towards Isola Piana in the distance. In the summer the place is mobbed, so you'll need to arrive extra early to grab a sliver of sand for your towel.

Isola di Asinara

Behind the deserted, *macchia*-blanketed Isola Piana is Isola di Asinara (donkey island), named after the world's only race of miniature albino donkeys which live here. At 17 km long by 6 km wide, Asinara is Sardinia's second-largest offshore island, yet aside from the donkeys, a few mouflon and pigs, it is completely uninhabited.

The island's remote location and harsh landscape of sharp cliffs and treeless shrub has shaped its odd history. It was used as a quarantine station for cholera victims in 1861, as a penal colony from 1885, and as a maximum security prison for Red Brigade and Mafia members until 1997 when it became a national park.

Today the park is a popular excursion for divers, trekkers and those looking to spot the snow-white, dwarf donkeys. Visitors dock at **Fornelli** at Asinara's southern point where guides are on hand to whisk tourists around on sightseeing trains or by bus to one of the park's three beaches at **Cala D'Oliva** in the northeast, where they can join other tours.

Impretours run ferries from Stintino's **Porto Mannu** ① *T079-508024, Easter-Sep daily 0930 and 1530, €12*, and from **Porto Torres** ① *near the Aragonese tower, T079-508042, 0830 and 1500, €12*, to Asinara. Fara (T348-472 2562) runs buses from the dock at Fornelli to Cala D'Oliva; call ahead to reserve tickets. It's possible to tour Asinara without a guide but, in the summer with soaring temperatures and no shade, we don't recommend it. You should also bring your own food and water, as there are no shops.

Castelsardo and around → *For listings, see pages 66-74.*

In the 12th century the Genoese Doria family dreamed of establishing a fortified settlement near Alghero to ensure political and economic control of northwest Sardinia. In hindsight, if they wanted to keep invaders out, they probably shouldn't have chosen one of the island's most dramatically beautiful settings as its location. Instead, they built Castelgenovese above a rocky promontory overlooking the Gulf of Asinara, with a medieval town rising like a wave up to a castle at its summit, and the sharp hillside breaking below. Sure enough, unwelcome visitors were soon knocking at the door and, by 1448, Castelgenovese had been renamed Castelaragonese after its new owners. Like in much of Sardinia, Aragonese rule led to a subsequent decline marked by rampant malaria outbreaks and pirate raids in the town. The Savoyards changed the town's name again to Castelsardo in 1769, and Ligurian immigrants introduced the town to its thriving fish and lobster industry. Today, Castelsardo remains understandably popular with visitors. A modern residential neighbourhood has grown up below the castle but the town's residents retain many of their age-old traditions, particularly the production of fine hand-woven baskets.

Medieval Castelsardo
Visitors arrive in Castelsardo's lower, modern district, which is chock-full of restaurants and tourist emporiums. All roads lead up from the central piazza della Pianedda to the medieval district: you can either climb the steep steps up via Trieste or drive up via Nazionale.

Fortezza dei Doria crowns Castelsardo at its highest point. Built by the Dorias in 1102, the castle housed Eleonora d'Arborea when her brother, Ugone III, was killed in 1383, forcing her to take over as *giudicessa* of Arborea. The fortress has outlived its defensive purpose and now holds the **Museo dell'Intreccio** ① *T079-471380, Mon-Sat 0930-1300 and 1500-1830, €2, €1 children*, dedicated to Sardinia's ancient basket- and wicker-weaving traditions. The castle culminates at the terrace with sky-high views of Castelsardo and the entire gulf below. Outside, it's not uncommon to see women sitting in their doorways weaving palm leaves into baskets.

Via Seminario connects the medieval district's two churches: the 16th-century **Chiesa di Santa Maria**, famous for its 13th-century black crucifix, and the **Cattedrale di Sant'Antonio Abate**, which is dwarfed by its octagonal campanile. The Dorias originally designed the soaring tower as a lighthouse and later topped it with a multi-hued majolica dome. The church's highlight is a Baroque painting above the main altar of the Madonna with six angels by the enigmatic 'Maestro di Castelsardo'. Sant'Antonio Abate's foundations rest on top of an early Romanesque structure, which is partially visible in the crypt as part of the **Museo Diocesano Cripte** ① *Jun-Aug daily 1030-1300 and 1830-2400, €2*.

Roccia dell'Elefante
Three-and-a-half kilometres southeast of Castelsardo, where the SS134 and SS200 meet, you can't miss the red trachyte Elephant Rock, so called because its wind-eroded 'trunk' nearly hangs over the road. A closer look reveals several *domus de janas* tombs hollowed out of the Elephant's base by the Ozieri Culture in about 3500 BC. If you crouch down, you'll see two bull's horns carved into either side.

Nuraghe Paddaggiu and Valledoria

From the Elephant, take the SS200 exit towards the pleasant coastal town of Valledoria. Slow down as you ride under the overpass and look for a dirt path soon after on the left from which to admire Nuraghe Paddaggiu. You can't visit Paddaggiu (haystack, in Sardo), but a landscaping crew of gazing sheep provides a quintessentially "Sardinian" photo-op.

Seven kilometres on, the coastal beachtown of Valledoria is the best bathing option near Castelsardo – though the Castelsardesi just swim off their own rocky coast. A 10-km beach stretches east from here to Isola Rossa, changing names as it goes: the most popular section is **Baia Verde** near the town's entrance. Valledoria sits at the mouth of northern Sardinia's longest river, the Coghinas, which can be explored by kayak or canoe as a great way to beat the crowds (see page 73).

Anglona

Inland, the undulating farmland of the Anglona region was home to the first known Sardinians back in the Late Paleolithic Age (500,000 BC) but is sparsely populated today. With your own transportation you could easily see the following sights in a single day. Ten kilometres south of Castelsardo, Tergu's main attraction is the **Nostra Signora di Tergu** church. The site has always been a holy place – first as a Nuraghic temple, then a Roman temple, and later a monastery. The Pisans are responsible for the present medieval reincarnation: a 12th century Romanesque church built with red trachyte and outlined in white limestone. Two columns frame the façade's rose window, and a square campanile backs the structure. On via Nazionale is a massive limestone boulder containing a series of *domus de janas* burial tombs from the third millennium BC. The Spanish converted the mound into a prison and, when they left, it was used as a residence, right up until 2001. Today, the site houses an ethnographic display (via Nazionale 23, T349-844 0436, web.tiscali.it/sedini, Jun-Sep daily 0900-1300 and 1500-1800, or by appointment, donations welcome).

Continue east on the SS134 past Bulzi and look for the 12th-century Pisan-Romanesque **Chiesa di San Pietro di Simbranos** in an abandoned field to the left. A bas-relief on the façade shows a Benedictine abbot standing between bearded monks with his arms raised in prayer. Evidence of the area's earliest Paleolithic inhabitants is on display in Perfugas at the **Museo Archeologico e Paleobotanico** ① *via Sauro, T079-564241, Jun-Sep Tue-Sun 0900-1300 and 1600-2000, Oct-May Tue-Sun 0900-1300 and 1500-1900, €3*. The village also has a late Nuraghic well temple in its centre.

Sassari and the northwest listings

For hotel and restaurant price codes and other relevant information, see pages 11-17.

🛏 Where to stay

Sassari *p51, map p52*
€€ Frank Hotel, *Via Diaz 20, T079-276456, frankhotel.com*. Frank is the cheapest hotel in town and caters to the business crowd. Aesthetically, it's stuck in the '80s (note the crank phone in the hallway) but the rooms are perfectly fine and the breakfast buffet is small but appetizing. The bathroom is shoehorned in a closet-sized space and has a shower that's guaranteed to flood your floor.

€€ Vittorio Emanuele, *Corso Vittorio Emanuele 100/102, T079-235538, hotelvittorioemanuele.ss.it*. This is Sassari's nicest hotel, conveniently located a short walk from the train and bus stations. Set in a refurbished building on Sassari's main avenue, the rooms all come equipped with air-conditioning and private bath. The lobby's art gallery and the vaulted wine cellar add a touch of class.

€ **Casa Chiara**, *Vicolo Bertolinis 7, T079-200 5052, casachiara.net.* This is a great and affordable B&B in the centre of the medieval district. The second-floor of an 18th-century *palazzo* has been restored to offer three rooms sharing two baths. Guests may also use the kitchen.

The Logudoro *p56*

€ **Hotel Liberty**, *Piazza dei Poeti, Pattada, T079-755384, libertyhotelpattada.it.* Pattada's finest hotel has 11 modern rooms in an attractive art nouveau building from the 1920s. Each has a bright tiled bathroom, TV and air-conditioning. The restaurant downstairs makes its own *Pattadese* pasta and the local owner can point potential knife buyers in the right direction.

Alghero *p58, map p60*

€€€€ **Villa Las Tronas**, *Lungomare Valencia 1, T079-981818, villalastronas.com. 4-night min stay in summer.* Alghero's most prestigious hotel hosted Italian royalty until the 1940s and still feels like a palatial villa. Set on a rocky bluff jutting into the sea, Las Tronas retains the trappings of its regal past: antique beds, oriental rugs and mahogany chests. Add lush gardens, a pool and a spa, encircled by sweeping views of the sea, and this place is something else!

€€€ **Hotel Catalunya**, *Via Catalogna 24, T079-953172, hotelcatalunya.it.* This hotel has a no-fuss business-class feel about it but, with 128 air-conditioned rooms, you're likely to find space here when there's none elsewhere. Request a view towards Alghero's historic district.

€ **Aigua**, *Via Machin 22, T339-591 2476, algua.it.* This completely restored B&B in Alghero's historical district has three cosy apartments, each with air-conditioning and private bathroom, plus a shared downstairs kitchen. The delightful location and charm

more than make up for its low wooden ceilings and lack of lift.

€ **Hotel San Francesco**, *Via Machin 2, T079-980330, sanfrancescohotel.com.* This unique and central hotel is housed in a former 14th-century convent. The rooms have everything you need and not much else but many overlook the attractive cloistered courtyard below, where breakfast is served.

€ **Mamajuana**, *Vicolo Adami 12, T339-136 9791, mamajuana.it.* Found up a flight of steps on one of the old town's cobblestone side streets, this old building has been done-up and has four sunny rooms overlooking piazza Municipio. Never mind the small bathrooms and scant breakfast served out of a vending machine, you can't beat the price and the location.

Camping

€ **La Mariposa**, *Via Lido 22, T079-950360, lamariposa.it. Mar-Sep only.* One kilometre north of Alghero, La Mariposa is Sardinia's oldest campsite but remains one of its better ones. In addition to spaces for tents and campers, guests may book bungalows and small villas. The private beach, Internet access, bike rentals, kite, diving and windsurfing centre ensure the hours fly by.

Around Alghero *p61*

€€€€ **El Faro**, *Località Porto Conte, 10 km west of Alghero towards Punta del Giglio, T079-942010, elfarohotel.it. Apr-Oct only.* Set on a dramatic rocky outpost at the end of Porto Conte, this resort's stylish rooms overlook the calm bay below and face Capo Caccia. Guests have use of two pools and a spa, plus diving, sailing and other excursions.

€€€€ **Punta Negra**, *between Fertilia and Porto Conte, T079-930222, hotelpuntanegra. com. Apr-Oct only.* The elegant property borders its own private beach and has a pool and tennis courts. It's also affiliated to diving and windsurfing outfitters. All rooms have balconies but you'll want one with a view of the bay.

€ **Agriturismo Porticciolo**, *Località Porticciolo, Porto Conte, T079-918000, agriturismoporticciolo.it*. Signposted where the SS127 meets the road around Porto Conte, Porticciolo has cute bungalow-style apartments, each with its own kitchenette, upstairs loft, bathroom and air-conditioning. Meals are served in an enormous dining room where guests gorge on four courses by an open hearth.

The Nurra *p63*

€€€ **La Pelosetta**, *Località Capo Falcone, Stintino, T079-527188, lapelosetta.it. May-Oct only*. This sand-coloured building is steps away from La Pelosa with a view that's worth every penny. In addition to well-equipped standard rooms, guests may reserve apartments by the week.

€€ **Silvestrino**, *Via Sassari 14, Stintino, T079-523007, hotelsilvestrino.it. Mar-Nov only*. Silvestrino is a comfortable hotel that doesn't go overboard when it comes to amenities, so spend a few euros more and request air-conditioning. The panoramic terrace and the top-floor rooms have great views of the twin harbours but the restaurant is the stand-out attraction.

€ **Ostello Cala d'Oliva**, *Località Cala d'Oliva, Isola di Asinara, T346 173 7043, sognasinara.com. May-Oct only*. Asinara's park cooperative runs the island's only accommodation: a restaurant and modest hostel that's better suited to the adventurous than those seeking comfort. The hostel has a large terrace facing the sea and 110 beds, divided in to rooms of up to five people, each with its own shower.

Castelsardo and around *p65*

€€ **Hotel Riviera**, *Via Lungomare Anglona 1, Castelsardo, T079-470143, hotelriviera.net*. The Riviera is located below the rising old town across the street from Castelsardo's small beach. The modern rooms offer plenty of comfort and the restaurant downstairs is one of Castelsardo's best and most expensive seafood options.

€ **Casa Doria**, *Via Garibaldi 10, Castelsardo, T349-355 7882, casadoria.it*. If you can haul your bags up to Castelsardo's medieval district, the Casa Doria is an attractive option at one of Castelsardo's highest points. Three (rather dark) rooms share two bathrooms but the highlight is the upstairs breakfast room, with its thatched roof, fireplace and seaside views of the Gulf of Asinara.

€ **Eleonora d'Arborea**, *Via Garibaldi 19, Castelsardo, T347-605 4828, residenzaeleonoradarborea.it*. An elegantly restored B&B housed in a 13th-century building. There are three rooms and, while you can't go wrong with any of them, the best is the top-floor apartment with its own kitchen and balcony. Owner Martino is local and owns the food shop downstairs.

Camping

La Foce, *Via Ampurias 1, Valledoria, T079-582109, lafoce.eu. May-Sep only*. La Foce is set around eucalyptus trees at the mouth of the Coghinas river and steps from the beach. The bungalows and villa lodging options are quite refined. New Kayak Sardinia operates from here.

❓ Restaurants

Sassari *p51, map p52*

€€€€ **Il Cenacolo**, *Via Ozieri 2, T079-236251. Mon-Sat 1300-1430 and 2000-2230*. A chic affair with stiff white tablecloths and flickering candles by night. Seafood is Cenacolo's speciality, with several dishes incorporating *bottarga* or mussels.

€€€€ **L'Antica Hostaria**, *Via Cavour 55, T079-200066. Mon-Sat 1300-1430, 2000-2230*. This rust-red restaurant is run by two brothers and is Sassari's finest and most intimate eatery. Choose from mouth-watering bass served in broccoli sauce, rabbit filled with porcini mushrooms and thyme in a pumpkin sauce or orzo with shrimp.

€€€ **Trattoria Da Antonio**, *Via Arborea 2B, T079-234297. Mon-Sat 1230-1430 and 1930-*

2245. A rustic atmosphere pervades this revamped warehouse. Pasta is nowhere in sight but there are lots of secondi to choose from. The *cordula con piseli* is a *Sassarese* speciality: cow's intestines with onions and peas in a sauce.

€€ Trattoria L'Assassino, *Vicolo Ospizio Cappuccini 1A, T079-235041. Mon-Sat 1230-1500 and 2000-2230.* The Assassin is hidden in an alley near via Tola and loved by locals for its quality and fair prices. If there's two of you, opt for the 'Sassareseria' and sample eight typical dishes from Sassari for €18. The homemade *pane carasau* bread is addictive.

€ Pizzeria Cocco, *Via Rosello 25, T079-238052. Mon-Sat 1000-1300 and 1700-2100.* A take-away in Sassari's historic district with folded *pizzettas* and typical chickpea *faine*.

Cafés and bars

Caffè Roma, *Via Roma, T079-201 3003. Mon-Sat 0700-2130.* Café by day, swanky bar by night with modish types spilling out of its backlighted yellow interior onto the street.

Mocambo Caffè, *Via Roma 97, T348-999 8375. Mon-Sat 0730-2200.* A popular morning spot serving the standard bar fare plus delicious fresh orange juice.

The Logudoro *p56*

€€ L'Opera, *Piazza Garibaldi, Ozieri, T079 787026. Daily 1230-1430 and 1930-2245.* A surprise in the centre of Ozieri: a casual restaurant serving surf and turf inside a converted two-storey ballroom with frescoes covering the ceiling. The *gnochetti sardi* are tasty but stay away from the *agnello*.

Alghero *p58, map p60*

€€€€ Al Tuguri, *Via Maiorca 113, T079-976772. Mon-Sat 1930-2300.* Al Tuguri is one of Alghero's most famous luxury seafood restaurants and has intimate seating on three wood-panelled levels. Mullet, sea urchin, bass, squid, prawns and lobster are all served with Iberian flair, and there's delicious *crema catalana* for dessert.

€€€€ Il Pavone, *Piazza Sulis 3/4, T079-979584, Mon-Sat 1300-1500 and 2000-2230.* The Peacock is an *Algherese* staple, with elegant patio seating that overlooks the Torre Sulis. Choose from fish or meat, accompanied by Alghero's famous Sella & Mosca wine. Service is impeccable.

€€€€ La Lepanto, *Via Carlo Alberto 135, T079-979116. May-Sep daily, Oct-Apr Tue-Sun.* Chef Moreno Cecchini is one of Sardinia's most famous seafood chefs, although locals complain this place is not what it was since it came onto the tourist radar. Lobster is the star attraction: try it doused in orange sauce or, even better, with olive oil.

€€€ Al Refettorio, *Vicolo Adami 47, T079-731126. Mon-Sat 1230-1430 and 1900-2330.* This new kid on the *carrer* is Alghero's restaurant of the moment. There's chic indoor seating with mood lighting or outdoor dining under a covered walkway. The mixed grilled seafood is a meal in itself, and the *paella algherese* is delicious. The restaurant doubles as a great wine bar with lots of munchies.

€€€ La Posada del Mar, *Vicolo Adami 29. Mon-Sat 1230-1500 and 1900-2230.* Tables spill out onto the cobblestones from this upscale eatery. Choose from fixed menus at €18 and €28, or à la carte. The pasta and prawns dashed with saffron is good, but locals recommend the sea urchin.

Cafés and bars

Birreria Sant Miquel, *Via Ardoino 51. Tue-Sun 0900-1600 and 1900-0200.* Tables outdoors, chess boards indoors and lots of beer on tap. There are also wine, cocktails and sandwiches available.

Café del Corso, *Via Carlo Alberto 77, T079-975596. Daily 0800-0200.* The cascading oleanders and outdoor seating render this one of Alghero's most popular cafés, and the busy pedestrian thoroughfare makes for good people-watching.

Gelateria Arcobaleno, *Piazza Civico 33. Feb-Oct Thu-Mon 1100-2300, Tue-Wed 1300-*

2300. Very hyped, but this small gelateria lives up to its reputation as Alghero's best.

Around Alghero *p61*
€€€ Sa Mandra Agriturismo, *Località Sa Segada, Fertilia, T079-999150. Daily by reservation 1300-1500 and 1900-2200.* Rita, Mario and their two children operate this top-notch restaurant along the SP44 road north of the airport. All dishes come directly from the family's 100-ha farm and a typical meal is so plentiful (and delicious) that it's hard to pace yourself.

The Nurra *p63*
€€€€ Silvestrino, *Via Sassari 14, Stintino, T079-523007. Fri-Wed 1930-2230.* Outdoor seating under a veranda facing the water and attention to detail by head chef Efisio Denegri make this Stintino's best seafood restaurant. Try the lobster soup and *cozze gratinate* mussels accompanied by a glass of Sella & Mosca wine.
€€€ Capo Falcone, *Località Capo Falcone, Stintino, T079 527037. Daily 0900-2400, food served 1200-1500 and 1930-2300.* Located high above the cape, this restaurant/pizzeria has a two-level terrace overlooking La Pelosa beach. With a view like this, the food is often an afterthought, but the open grill serves some delicious steaks, and the seafood selection is impressive.

Cafés and bars
Lu Fanali, *Lungomare Colombo 89, Stintino, T079-523054. Daily 0730-2230, food served 1230-1430 and 1930-2200.* This cafè/pizzeria/bar has sublime patio seating directly on the water and serves snacks, salads, seafood and sweets.

Castelsardo *p65*
€€€€ Il Cormorano, *Via Colombo 7, T079-470628. Wed-Mon 1930-2230.* Locals say the Pinna brothers serve some of the best seafood dishes around. Especially popular is the marinated tuna, linguine with sea urchin, and spaghetti with Castelsardo lobster.

€€€€ La Guardiola, *Piazza del Bastione 4, T079-470428. Tue-Sun 1230-1400 and 1930-2300.* Castelsardo's most upscale restaurant occupies much of its finest real estate on piazza del Bastione. Whether you get a table inside or on the terrace, you're guaranteed amazing views of the coast. Pasta and meat dishes here are fine, but the Guardiola is known for its seafood.
€€€ La Trattoria, *Via Nazionale 20, T079-470661. Tue-Sun 1230-1430 and 1930-2230.* Pictures of shaggy old-time shepherds adorn the walls in this sophisticated but relaxed eatery. Chef Maria Giuseppa whips up *pane carasau* topped with onions, penne with crab and fantastic *zuppa gallurese* (by reservation).

🎭 Entertainment

Sassari *p51, map p52*
Clubs
Sergeant Pepper, *Via Asproni 20, T079-282805. Fri-Sun 2300-0400.* Sassari's most central disco plays mainly Latin and salsa music on Friday, and live hip-hop or house music on Saturday and Sunday.
Tumbao, *Largo Pazzola 11, T349-332 7913. Thu-Sat 2200-0300.* This club tucked into Sassari's historic district is private, but the owners are tourist-friendly. The bar is popular with the university crowd and plays a variety of music, from Latin to pop to jazz to Sardo folk.

Gay and lesbian
Time, *Via Civitavecchia 3/G. Tue-Sat 2100-0300.* A gay-friendly wine bar.

Alghero *p58, map p60*
Children
Trenino Catalano, *Porta a Mare, T336-691836. €5, €3 under-9s.* A tourist train whisks families through Alghero's historic district with (somewhat unintelligible) descriptions of the town's sights in English on this 20-minute tour.

Clubs
El Tró, *Lungomare Valencia 3, T079-973 3000. Fri-Sat 2300-0500.* A lively disco within walking distance of downtown Alghero. This attractive club is set on a rock jutting into the water, which helps justify its popularity (especially with tourists), high entrance fee and drink prices.

Performance
Teatro Civico, *Piazza Vittorio Emanuele, T079-973 1057.* Built in 1826, this is Sardinia's only wooden theatre and hosts frequent theatre productions and concerts.

Around Alghero *p61*
Clubs
Il Ruscello, *Località Angeli Custodi, T079-953168. Jun-Sep Thu-Sat 2300-0500.* One of the northeast's most popular discos is found 10 km north of Alghero toward Olmedo. The open-air club has two dance rooms separated by a large garden and specializes in house, techno and pop music.

The Nurra *p63*
Clubs
L'Isolotto, *Via Cala di Rena, Stintino, T079-523088. May-Sep Fri-Sat 2400-0500.* A bar/pizzeria but also Stintino's only disco. DJs spin dance music by the club's outdoor pool overlooking the sea.

🎉 Festivals and events

Sassari *p51, map p52*
On the second to last Sunday in May, thousands of Sardi in traditional dress convene in Sassari for the **Cavalcata Sarda**, a parade through the streets, followed by music and dancing.

Li Candaleri The most important date on Sassari's calendar is its thanksgiving celebration on 14 August, known as *Li Candaleri*. The festival honours the Virgin for allegedly saving the city from three plague epidemics between 1528 and 1652, each of which is said to have ended on 14 August.

To thank their protector, eight cand bearers from each of Sassari's nine medieval guilds (known as *Gremi*) haul a 5-m tall wooden 'candle' from piazza Castello to the Chiesa di Santa Maria di Betlem (see below). The candles weigh between 200 and 300 kg each and are festooned in flowers and ribbons. Children hold the ribbons and dance to the rhythm of drum beats and the tune of the *pifferario* flute. The parade stops in front of the Teatro Civico on corso Vittorio Emanuele, where Sassari's mayor greets the *Gremi* with the *Sassarese* expression "*A zent'anni!*" ("May you live a hundred years!"). The response is either applause, if he's governing well, or whistles, if not, and marks the start of the most important part of the procession, *Sa Faradda* ('the descent') down to the church. Traditionally, the farmers' Gremio was the most important guild, as the city depended on it for food, so they enter the church first. Once inside, each guild places its candles around the image of the Virgin and a city-wide celebration of music and feasting ensues.

Porto Torres and around *p54*
In early May pilgrims from throughout northwestern Sardinia walk to Porto Torres' San Gavino church for **Festha Manna**, to pray for the three martyred saints, Gavino, Proto and Gianuario.

The Logudoro *p56*
Ozieri commerates the summer solstice with a bonfire on 23 June. It also celebrates the **Festa della Madonna del Rimedio** at the end of September to thank the Virgin for ridding the town of the plague. The religious festival is followed by the Su Cantaru and *Cantareddu* choral and poetry competition.

Alghero *p58, map p60*
Known as **San Christus dei Jermans Blancs**, Alghero's Easter rites are steeped in Catalan influence. On the Tuesday before

...essione dei Misteri (Passion ...eaves from San Francesco ...wed by the parade of a 17th-...oden cross. On Good Friday, four m... ...emove the nails from a statue of Jesus and on Easter Sunday, it is paraded through the streets. Other events on the calendar include the **Sagra del Riccio Mare** (sea urchin harvest) in early March and an international classical music festival, **Estate Musicale**, in July and August.

Castelsardo and around *p65*

Easter is a decidedly Spanish-themed affair in Castelsardo. On Good Friday, hooded men enact a mock funeral for Christ, while on Easter Monday, the **Lunissanti** procession travels from Castelsardo to Tergu for a torch-lighting ceremony at Nostra Signora church.

○ Shopping

Sassari *p51, map p52*
Antica Salumeria Mangatia, *Via Università 68, T079-234710. Mon-Fri 0830-1330 and 1700-2000, Sat 0830-1330.* Sells a myriad of fresh cheeses, pastas and meats from around the island, including *panadas* packed with meat from Montiferru's *bue rosso* bulls.

The Logudoro *p56*
Pasticceria Pinna Pietro, *Via Pastorino 35, Ozieri, T079-787451. Mon-Sat 0900-1200 and 1630-1900.* Ozieri is known for its handmade desserts, especially *sospiri* (sighs), made from almond paste and covered in sugar, chocolate or myrtle.
Piero Fogarizzu, *Via Belvedere, Pattada, T079-754137. By appointment only.* Piero comes from four generations of *pattadese* knife-makers and is considered one of Sardinia's top craftsmen. He typically works only by custom order and pays for shipping within Italy. International shipping costs are split with the customer.

Alghero *p58, map p60*
DeFilippi's, *Via Roma 41, T079-978100. Apr-Oct daily 0930-2100, Nov-Mar daily 0930-1300 and 1630-2000.* Lots of blood-red coral in necklace, earring and bracelet form plus watches and turquoise jewellery. English-speaking staff.
Explora, *Via Carlo Alberto 65, T079-981991. Mon-Sat 0930-1300 and 1630-2000.* There's a little of everything Sardinian in this one-stop souvenir shop: crafts, wine, sweets, cheese, *bottarga*, cork, knives… you name it, it's here!
Il Labirinto, *Via Carlo Alberto 119, T079-980496. Daily 0900-1330 and 1500-2100.* A classic bookshop with a few English-language novels and some beautiful black-and-white photography books showing Sardinia in the 1950s.

Castelsardo *p65*
Tutto Artigianato, *Via Roma 31, T079-471266. Mon-Sat 0900-1330 and 1500-2000.* A wonderful place to purchase Castelsardo's trademark handmade baskets. Upstairs, hand-woven rugs from throughout Sardinia are sold.

○ What to do

Alghero *p58, map p60*
Andrea Jensen, *T338-970 8139, ajsailing. com. €75 per person, €35 children.* Cruise around coastal Alghero aboard a 1930s yacht. The bilingual crew pick you up from the port in the morning, whisk you around Capo Caccia, past prime dolphin-spotting waters where you stop for snorkelling and lunch made fresh on the boat, before sailing back to town. With a usual quota of just 12 people, this is spectacular!
NautiSub, *Via Garibaldi 45, T079-952433, nautisub.com.* Bilingual staff run full- and half-day dive trips to Capo Caccia and Nereo's Cave, all starting from €38.
Pintadera, *Vicolo Adami 41, T079-917064, pintadera.info.* Wine tasting, Italian courses and cooking lessons in the heart of Alghero.

Stroll & Speak, *Via Cavour 4, T339-489 9314, strollandspeak.com.* Learn Italian from locals while walking around Alghero.

Around Alghero *p61*
Capo Galera Diving Center, *Località Capo Galera, southwest of Lazzaretto, T079-942110, capogalera.com.* This well-established dive operator runs dozens of training courses and submersions around the Rivieria del Corallo, including the fantastic Nereo's Cave. Single dives start at €20. Keen divers will want to stay at the centre's fabulous villa hotel overlooking the sea.

The Nurra *p63*
Asinara Diving Center, *Porto dell'Ancora, Stintino, T079-527000, asinaradivingcenter.it.* Locals say this is your best bet for diving in Asinara's protected marine park. It also offers dives around Capo Falcone and runs courses for adults and children as young as eight.
Windsurfing Center Stintino, *Località L'Approdo, Stintino, T079-527006, windsurfingcenter.it.* This top-notch outfitter is on Le Saline beach, offering windsurfing, sailing and diving lessons, boat hire and day-long excursions to Asinara aboard three 40-foot catamarans.

Castelsardo and around *p65*
New Kayak Sardinia, *Camping La Foce, Via Ampurias 1, Valledoria, T338-125 8403, newkayaksardinia.it.* This outfit offers guided or individual kayak, canoe and paddle-boat excursions down the River Coghinas (by reservation). The three routes last between three and six hours (€19-22) and cut through the north coast's undeveloped countryside, past Roman ruins, juniper trees and canyons.

⊖ Transport

Sassari *p51, map p52*
Sassari is built on a long, walkable slope with the modern development to the east and the medieval quarter to the west. A single road that changes names from via Roma to largo Cavalotti to corso Vittorio Emanuele passes a series of piazzas, joining the new to the old. Up to nine ARST buses daily run between Alghero-Fertilia airport and Sassari's bus station (30 mins). Local ATP buses to Platamona beach depart from the Giardini Pubblici.

The bus station, **Stazione Bus**, is on via XXV Aprile, T079-263 9203, T079-241301.

The train station, **Stazione Ferroviaria**, is on piazza Stazione, T079-260362, T079-245740, trenitalia.com.

There are frequent daily ARST buses to Porto Torres (30 mins) and Alghero (30 mins), plus up to seven daily to Torralba (50 mins-1hr 40 mins), one to Olbia (1 hr 30 mins), four to Bosa (2 hrs 15 mins) and two to Cagliari (3 hrs 30 mins). Up to four daily trains run from Sassari to Cagliari (2 hrs 50 mins to 3 hrs 45 mins), 10 to Alghero (30 mins) and seven to Olbia (2 hrs). Most routes require passengers to change at Ozieri-Chilivani.

Alghero *p58, map p60*
You can only drive through Alghero's medieval centre from 0800 to 1030 and from 1430 to 1630, but its small size means it's easy to explore on foot. From via Cagliari, up to 19 AIFA buses run daily to Alghero Airport, 12 km away (30 mins), and frequent AO buses go along the coast, all the way to Capo Caccia (50 mins). There are also three daily buses from Alghero to the Sella & Mosca vineyards (20 mins).

The ARST bus station, **Stazione Bus**, is on Giardini Pubblici, ARST T079-950179, FdS T079-950458. Up to 15 ARST buses travel daily from Alghero's via Catalogna to Sassari (1 hr), eight to Porto Torres (1 hr) and two to Bosa (1 hr).

The train station, **Stazione Ferroviaria**, is on via Don Minzoni, 2 km north of Alghero centre, T079-950785, trenitalia.com. Up to 11 daily trains go to Sassari (35 mins) where you can change for trains to Cagliari.

Castelsardo *p65*

Up to 14 daily ARST buses travel from Castelsardo to Sassari (1 hr) and four stop at Valledoria (25 mins) en route to Santa Teresa di Gallura (1 hr 40 mins).

Directory

Sassari *p51, map p52*

Money There are three banks in piazza Italia where you can change or withdraw money. **Medical services** For emergency assistance, contact Sassari's **Guardia Medica** (ambulance/emergency response) on T079-206 2222 to be taken to various medical emergency sites. Pharmacy at via Roma 14 (Mon-Fri 0915-1300 and 1630-2000, Sat 0915-1300). **Post office Poste Italiane**, via Brigata Sassari 19, T079-234380 (Mon-Fri 0800-1850, Sat 0800-1315).

Tourist information Teatro Civico, corso Vittorio Emanuele 35, T331-437 7156 (Mon-Fri 0900-1400 and 1500-1800).

Alghero *p58, map p60*

Money Banca Nazionale del Lavoro and **MPS Banca** are next to each other at No 5 and No 11 via Vittorio Emanuele. **Medical services** Hospital: **Ospedale Civile**, via Don Minzoni, 2 km north of Alghero centre, T079-996200. Pharmacy: **Farmacia Bulla**, via Garibaldi 13, T079-952115 (Mon-Sat 0915-1300 and 1630-2000). **Post office Poste Italiane**, via Carducci 35, T079-972 0200 (Mon-Fri 0800-1800, Sat 0800-1300). **Tourist information** The main office is at piazza Porta Terra 9, T079-979054 (Mon-Sat 0800-2000, Sun 1000-1300). An additional office is located in the Torre di Porta Terra.

Contents

Footprint features

Nuoro & Ogliastra

Sardinia's rebellious character springs from its interior, a rugged patchwork of villages hemmed in by the Gennargentu and Supramonte mountain massifs on two sides and the sea on the other. A large swathe of this territory comprises the Gennargentu National Park, which extends from the Supramonte east to the Golfo di Orosei and remains one of the most remote and impenetrable pockets in the Mediterranean. Despite nearly 3000 years of invaders, this region has only been conquered in name. The Romans raided it 15 times but failed to subdue the area, dubbing it 'Barbarie' after the barbarian-like ferocity and customs of its inhabitants. The name has stuck as 'Barbagie', the collective name for a cluster of five groups of rural communities: Nuoro, Ollolai, Mandrolisai, Belvì and Seulo. And, even today, Italian street signs are often ripped through by bullet holes, while those in Sardo are left untouched.

Central Sardinia is brimming with unparalleled beauty. You won't find more imposing peaks than the Gennargentu mountains or more mesmerizing beaches than along the Golfo di Orosei. Many of the cinderblock towns folded into the hills are softened by poignant *murales* and, as you explore these provinces, you will experience the island's warmest hospitality.

The Barbagie's capital, Nuoro, remains a strange melting pot, in which African street vendors mingle with old women in traditional dress who cross themselves after crossing the road. In the past, Nuoro produced so many gifted writers (including Nobel laureate, Grazia Deledda) that it was once known as the 'Athens of Sardinia'. But since it was upgraded to the provincial capital in 1926, Nuoro has fallen victim to the same unsightly development that blighted much of urban Italy in the 20th century.

The area north of Nuoro and west of Siniscola is a rugged expanse of winding valleys whose cork trees shade free-range livestock under the twin peaks of Monte Albo (1127 m). Most tourists overlook this region because of its utter remoteness and rollercoaster turns but, as long as you're not in dire need of a toilet or a bed, the gorgeous backdrop is worth the hassle. Just be sure to set out on a full tank of petrol and not a full stomach.

Nuoro

At its heart, this municipal city is just a small town overgrown by government that still turns to Deledda for inspiration: look for excerpts of her writing scattered around the streets. While the cradle of *Sardità* may have received a suburban makeover, it hasn't strayed far from its roots and you'll stumble upon some of Sardinia's most staunch traditionalists and finest museums here.

Nuoro's older districts, **Santu Predu** and **Seuna**, are stacked towards the top of the mountainous crater that holds the town, with the newer development falling below. Historically, the Santu Predu neighbourhood at the top of the hill was occupied by shepherds, while the less wealthy farmers lived in the Seuna quarter.

Older *Nuoresi* remember that the two quarrelling factions would only meet on corso Garibaldi in the commercial district that connected the two areas and that the shepherds used to hurl stones at the farmers below. ('Predu' derives from the Sardo word for stone.)

These days, **corso Garibaldi** is a more peaceful buffer and Nuoro's most attractive thoroughfare. The street's outdoor cafés are a prime spot to take in an afternoon espresso or an evening drink. Just off the corso is Sardinia's most serious contemporary art museum: **MAN** ① *via Satta 27, T0784-252110, museoman.it, Tue-Sun 1000-1300 and 1630-2030, €3, €2 concessions, free children and over-65s*, which has two floors displaying over 350 paintings and sculptures from Sardinia's premier 20th-century artists, plus frequent temporary exhibits.

Nuoro's detailed, if small, **Museo Archeologico** ① *via Mannu 1, T0784-31688, Wed and Fri-Sun 0900-1330, Tue and Thu 0900-1330 and 1500-1730, free*, is nestled near piazza San Giovanni and holds a variety of finds from the province's chief archaeological sites, ranging from an ancient skull of the monkeys that once roamed Sardinia, to *bronzetti* figurines and Roman coins.

Past the loud crimson gleam of the neoclassical **Cattedrale di Santa Maria della Neve**, via Mereu climbs the hill to shady **Parco di Sant'Onofrio** and the **Museo della Vita e delle Tradizioni Popolare** ① *via Mereu 56, T0784-31426, mid Jun-Sep daily 0900-2000, Oct-mid Jun daily 0900-1300 and 1500-1900, €3*. Inside, galleries are dedicated to the Barbagie's bizarre Carnival celebrations (see page 80). Some of the island's earliest instruments are also on display. Yet, it's the parade of traditional Sardinian dress that steals the show. A glass case full of mannequins shows off the island's elaborately embroidered peacock-coloured costumes and filigree jewellery, which were common everyday wear until the mid 20th century. The costumes from each area are each subtly different: Desulo's sunny colours look vaguely Eastern European, while Oliena's black-fringed headwraps dangle like hair; Aggius' heavy female cloaks nearly cover the face underneath, and Macomer's male costumes look just like *Carabinieri* uniforms.

Monte Ortobene

Nuoro's playground lies 6 km away at Monte Ortobene (955 m), which has beautiful views over the Supramonte and the Lanaittu valley (see page 81). At the peak, there's a shady ilex forest with picnic tables, a jungle-gym for the kids and a few pizzerias for the famished.

In 1900, the mountain was chosen by Pope Leone XIII as one of 19 throughout Italy to receive a giant bronze statue of Christ. The statue was unveiled on 29 August 1900 and thousands of Sardinians flocked to Nuoro to catch the spectacle. The tradition has stuck, and every year on 29 August, a procession of colourfully clad islanders parade through Nuoro and up to the statue in the **Processione del Redentore**. Follow signs for 'Redentore' past trickling fountains to reach the 7-m statue.

Su Tempiesu

ⓘ *Off the SS389, north of Nuoro, T328-756 5148, archeologiaviva.it. Daily 0900-1900, €3.*
Su Tempiesu is a well temple built with startling architectural precision for the worship of water from the 11th to the eighth centuries BC. It's the area's most fascinating Nuraghic monument and doubles as Nuoro's most scenic picnic spot.

Follow the brown signs north on the SS389 from Nuoro towards Orune before turning down a 7-km paved road to the ticket office and picnic area, which enjoys unbeatable views of the limestone massifs of Monte Albo. Two trails – take the 'Sentiero Faunistico' to pass two reconstructed Nuraghic huts – lead to the temple nestled between two canyon walls. Water from the chasm is channelled into a well under a triangular vestibule and trickles down a canal into a second basin when the spring overflows. Worshippers left votive *bronzetti* statues to the water gods on the two benches inside the atrium and studded the cornice with ornamental daggers. The entire structure is built in colourful trachyte and basalt rocks, which are found no fewer than 30 km away, and remains fully functioning 3100 years later: proof of the mysterious builders' architectural know-how and opulence.

Siniscola and the coast

Beyond Su Tempiesu, the mountain road continues past Bitti and signs for Lula and Lodè, corkscrewing as it climbs between the peaks of Monte Albo. Enjoy the views before, finally, snaking down to Siniscola, surrounded by citrus groves. To the east, the beaches along the coastal strip are popular getaways. **La Caletta** has a cluster of hotels and restaurants and some great birdwatching along its marshy canals to the south. Yet locals prefer the bathing spots south of **Santa Lucia**, off the SS125. The best of these is **Berchida**, found at the end of a long dirt road at km 242. In July and August, buy a €4 car park pass at Agriturismo Su Meriacru towards the beach.

Macomer and around

West of Nuoro, the province juts out around the granite plateau of Macomer. The town developed under the Romans as a junction along the Cagliari–Porto Torres road and remains the crossroads of Sardinia's public transport network. If you have your own transport, you probably won't want to bother with Macomer's centre but you could spend a full day driving around the archaeological sites in its environs.

Ten kilometres east of Macomer at Silanus, the **Santa Sabina** site has a strikingly well preserved single-tower nuraghe from the 14th century BC, with a climbable spiral staircase inside. A few steps away, its Christian descendant, a 10th-century Byzantine church built in black-and-white stones, is fringed by crouching *cumbessiàs* pilgrim houses, which are inhabited during a nine-day *novena* in September. Heading towards Macomer from here, the SS129 passes a graveyard of crumbling nuraghi.

Just off Highway 131 at km 144 north of Macomer, is the turnoff for **Nuraghe Santa Barbara**. A 15-minute walk from the car park will bring you to this reddish bastion whose central tower is all that remains of a four-lobed fortress. From the hillside, you can see the slanting **Nuraghe Ruiu** across the highway below.

The Supramonte → *For listings, see pages 89-95.*

North of the granite Gennargentu mountain range (meaning 'silver gate', because of its shiny schist gleam), Cannonau vineyards erupt into the bald limestone peaks of the Supramonte. This was once a notorious bandit hideout, covered with thick forests until the Piedmontese cut the holm and oak woods to build Italy's railroads in the 1800s. Even without its leafy coat, the Supramonte and the unspoiled Lanaittu valley still keep a tight hold of their secrets, sheltering archaeological sites, karstic caves and mountain sinkholes – not to mention Sardinia's most famous bandit, the 'Scarlet Rose'. The villages in this area boast Sardinia's most famous costumes: elderly women in Oliena still walk the street in black dresses embroidered with peacock colours and, if you plan your visit right, you may also stumble upon the sheepskin tunics worn during Mamoiada's otherworldly Carnival celebrations.

Mamoiada

At first glance, this lethargic enclave looks like any rural Italian village: rows of vineyards dot the rolling countryside and old men huddle together on park benches. But look a little closer and, along the main street, you'll see a handful of *murales* depicting the woolly ghouls of Mamoiada's *Mamuthones* carnival procession, see below.

If you can't make it to the village during Carnival, you can still learn about the Barbagie's pagan rites at the town's **Museo delle Maschere Mediterraneo** ① *piazza Europa 15, T0784-569018, museodellemaschere.it, daily 0900-1300 and 1500-1900, €4, €2.60 concessions.* You can also browse an impressive collection of the devilish disguises at Signor Mameli's workshop, **Maschere Mameli** (see page 93).

Orgosolo

Orgosolo has long held the distinguished title of bandit capital of Sardinia. During the first half of the 20th century, bus hold-ups were a regular occurrence and a murder took place every two months, leading director Vittorio de Seta to immortalize the town in his 1961 film, *I Banditi a Orgosolo*. Since then, the shepherding community has softened its image and is now more famous for Sardinia's first *murales* movement, which started in 1975 to mark the 30th anniversary of the Italian liberation from Fascism.

Orgosolo's cinderblock buildings are dressed with roughly 120 politically charged murals, rendered with precision and laced with captions in *Sardo*. Most are found along corso Repubblica and its side streets, and deal with the struggle to end corruption, violence and greed in an area which has long been a victim of all three. The murals also reflect a range of international events, from the slaying of Palestinian Mohammed

Carnival in the Barbagie

Unlike the light-hearted Christian revelry of Carnival celebrations on the mainland, the moving processions in Mamoiada (see page 79) and Ottana (see page 84) reflect the hardships of Sardinia's impoverished centre and remain gripped in mysterious pagan practices.

In Mamoiada, residents don menacing jet-black masks (sas viseras) made from dyed wild pear and alder wood, dark sheepskin tunics (sas peddhes), up to 30 kg of cowbells (sos sonazzos) and the rattling thighbones of sheep to transform themselves into the Mamuthones. These heavy beasts process through the streets, dragging their hunched frames forwards in two rows before breaking into synchronized convulsions. They are led by white-masked herders called Issohadores who guide them out of town while attempting to lasso any women in the crowd as an omen of fertility. (According to tradition, if an Issohadore accidentally ropes a man, the captured male has to buy drinks for all his companions!)

The exact meaning and origin of the Mamuthones procession has been lost over time and continues to baffle anthropologists. Roman invaders thought the beasts represented some kind of pagan animal worship and tried to outlaw them, but to no avail. The most accepted theory is that the Mamuthones represent the evil beings from the underworld that haunted Mamoiada's ancestors; the Issohadores capture these menacing spirits and drive them out of town in a pseudo-exorcism. In a post-Christian Barbagie, the rite has received a Catholic makeover and is now performed in January in honour of San Antonio Abate and again on Carnival Sunday.

In the town of Ottana, the Carnival procession also springs from the remote past and is probably rooted in Greek purification rites. Known as the Sos Merdules Bezzos, it evokes the struggle of man to keep from turning into the beasts he fights to tame. The procession's protagonist is Su Boe, a shaggy sheepskin-clad man draped in bells and covered in an elaborately horned mask representing an ox. The ox battles for dominance with herders, called Sos Merdules, each of whom wears a black mask depicting a beleaguered and fatigued expression. The herders' wives, Sas Filanzanas, follow their husbands, knitting wool all the way.

Al'Durra by Israeli forces, to the condemnation of Spanish dictator Francisco Franco, to the extermination of Native Americans by white settlers.

Despite the makeover, Orgosolo has yet to shake off its past. Many of the murals' verses were penned by town poet Peppino Marotto, who was shot dead in 2007. His murder allegedly stemmed from a vendetta dating back to the 1950s.

Oliena

Oliena enjoys a picture-perfect setting under the limestone wall of Monte Corrasi (1463 m). Its backdrop drew Italian bard Gabriele d'Annunzio in 1909, who came here to drink as much Cannonau wine as possible. He was so impressed with the wine that he wrote an article about it in the Corriere della Sera newspaper, urging readers to follow suit. His rapture propelled Oliena's Nepente label to international fame and it remains among Sardinia's most esteemed brands.

The Jesuits left their mark in the 17th century by building the bulky **Chiesa di Saint Ignazio** on Oliena's main street and introducing the population to silk worms. These still provide the thread for the elegantly embroidered black *muncadores* shawls worn by Oliena's elderly women, who walk the streets in conservative headwraps and ankle-length dresses.

Valle del Lanaittu

East of Oliena, the U-shaped Lanaittu valley is one of Sardinia's truly unspoiled highlights. Although it's ringed by the steep white walls of the Supramonte, the valley is surprisingly accessible and you could easily pass days among its fascinating nooks.

Five kilometres beyond Oliena towards Dorgali, turn off the road at signs for 'Su Gologone'. A short distance past the hotel of the same name (one of Sardinia's best, see page 89), you'll see an oasis of eucalyptus trees marking the entrance to the **Sorgente Su Gologone**. It's a magical spot with weeping willows billowing above the river Cedrino. Wooden signs point the way towards a 107-m deep spring that pushes 236 litres of water per second through a narrow crevice dug between a cleft in two vertical rock walls. In the winter, the spring water floods the surrounding knoll; in summer, it slows considerably and you can see fish feeding in the deep, crystal-clear pool.

Across the road from the park is the turn-off for the Lanaittu valley, 7 km away. The asphalt turns to dirt after 2 km and a fork in the road leads left to Tiscali and right to Sa Sedda 'e Sos Carros and to the **Su Bentu** ('the wind') and **Sa Oche** ('the voice') caves, so-called because of the surging wind and water that flows out of them after heavy rain. The limestone grottoes are filled with internal lakes, fed by a river deep in the Supramonte, and, although not fully surveyed, are thought to be among the deepest fissures in Europe. You will need spelunking experience to explore the caves; contact **Cooperative Ghivine** (see page 94), to find out more.

Buy tickets at the lodge next to the caves to visit the nearby Nuraghic village, **Sa Sedda 'e Sos Carros** ① *T347-824 9517, May-Nov daily 0930-1300 and 1500-1730, €4*. Ongoing excavations are busy uncovering the 200 huts that lie underground but what is visible is impressive enough. The village must have been the height of Bronze Age urban sophistication: dozens of *bronzetti* statues have been recovered here and the whole place benefited from a plumbing system that fed water from a cistern in the site's centre via conduits into each stone hut. The site's jewel, however, is the world's earliest constructed fountain, built using five different coloured stones. Water is channelled down a canal and shoots out of seven limestone mouths into a pool. Remarkably, the whole thing still works!

The Supramonte's most famous site is undoubtedly the **Villaggio Nuragico di Tiscali** ① *daily 0800-sunset, €5, €2 concessions*. The site is reached by climbing a loosely-laid rocky trail up the side of Monte Tiscali with breathtaking views of vertical limestone dolomites, dyed rust-red by erosion, and of the Lanaittu valley below. After nearly three hours, you descend into a fissure to find the scant remains of an ancient village hidden inside the depths of a giant sinkhole that has partially caved in. It's a moving sight, although the lack of excavation has left more questions than answers about its origins. What is known is that, while the Nuraghic population undoubtedly utilized the site, the present huts are the work of much later generations. The widely held theory is that Tiscali's utter inaccessibility is no accident, since it represented the last defensive refuge of a besieged native population forced further and further into Sardinia's depths to escape Carthaginian and Roman invaders.

There are two ways to hike to Tiscali: the first is to head a few kilometres south of Dorgali on the SS125 and turn left at the brown sign indicating 'Gola Gorroppu.' Follow the arrows towards Gola Gorroppu on the paved road for roughly 10 km, looking for signs to Tiscali. A steeper, slightly shorter and more scenic route is to follow the signs from the Valle del Lanaittu. This path is poorly marked and we strongly recommend using a guide. The lodge where you buy tickets to visit Sos Carros leads daily treks to Tiscali and is conveniently placed near the site but the guide doesn't speak English. Non-Italian speakers should call one of the companies on page 94.

Golfo di Orosei → For listings, see pages 89-95.

Some of Sardinia's most unforgettable beaches are found where the provinces of Nuoro and Ogliastra meet along the seaside section of the Gennargentu National Park, known as the Golfo di Orosei. Less is more on this dazzling stretch of unadulterated coastline, where the only high-rises are the limestone cliffs and you won't find a road or building for 40 km.

Orosei

At the head of the gulf is Orosei, a beachside resort backed by mountains. Its pleasant, almost Spanish feel comes courtesy of wealthy Aragonese barons, who ruled the surrounding area (known as 'Baronie') from the 16th to the 18th centuries, erecting churches and planting citrus groves when not warding off malaria outbursts.

Orosei's centrepiece is the leafy **piazza del Popolo**. A flight of steps next to the tourist office leads to the town's most famous landmark, the **Chiesa di San Giacomo**, built by the Pisans and restored with Spanish flair in the 18th century. The church's three tiled domes and campanile look vaguely Moorish. San Giacomo shares the square with one of the other ten churches packed into the town, the impressive **Oratorio del Rosario**, which has three crosses tacked on to its sun-baked façade. Nearby, **piazza Sas Animas** boasts an oratory church of the same name and the stout **Prione Vezza** tower which, as its name suggests, was a prison left over from a 14th-century castle.

Marina di Orosei

A walking and cycling path is laid along the flat 3-km stretch east of Orosei to its beach, Marina di Orosei, a scenic spot flanked by a narrow canal with views stretching across the entire gulf. At 5 km long, there's always towel space at the beach, whose name changes from Su Barone to Isporoddai to Osalla as you go south. From May to September, boats leave from the Marina's northern end – the same port that saw DH Lawrence off to Sicily in 1921– to cruise the Golfo di Orosei (see below). A more isolated bathing option is 13 km up the SS125 at **Biderrosa**. This beach is part of a protected park and only 120 cars are allowed in daily, even during peak season. Passes are sold on site and cost €10 per car plus €1 per person.

Cruising the Golfo di Orosei

Sardinia's most spectacular coastline is only accessible by boat. The Golfo di Orosei stretches for 70 km, dipping to form a crescent moon along Sardinia's eastern seaboard between Punta Nera in the north and Capo Monte Santu in the south. The 40-km stretch south of Cala Gonone is completely void of civilization and characterized by vertical limestone cliffs plunging head-first into deep grottoes and by hidden beaches with water that encompasses a palette of blues, from azure to indigo. This area is one of the gems of the Mediterranean and guaranteed to be a highlight of your trip.

From May to October tour boats cruise the gulf daily, leaving from the ports at **Cala Gonone** (see page 84) and **Santa Maria Navarrese** (see page 87). Most run from morning until evening with lunch on board and begin at around €30 a person. The boats get crowded in peak season, so avoid the less expensive ferry services that pack up to 200 people aboard and spend a bit more to ensure comfort. Pack sandals as the pebbly beaches can be tough on the feet.

South of Cala Gonone, the first stop is the M-shaped double-arched entrance to the **Grotte del Bue Marino** ⓘ *T0784-96243, Easter-Oct, book through the boat tour company,* named after one of the planet's most endangered mammals, the monk seal, which used to live in the cave's environs but has all but disappeared since the 1980s. A wooden walkway takes visitors along the cave's southern route, which, unlike the northern end, remains geologically active thanks to an underwater river. Stalactites and stalagmites abound and extend for a kilometre in the cave's saltwater lake. Look out for the Neolithic drawings showing humans dancing around a solar disc.

The coast's most famous beach, Cala Luna, is a short sail south. While you could easily pass a day lounging on its pebbly shoreline and exploring its caverns, the beach's most striking aspect is behind the shore, where flowering oleander bushes shelter a stream, forming a tranquil escape from the throngs of sun worshippers. Look for one of the last nesting spots of the elusive Eleonora falcon between **Cala Luna** and lovely **Cala Sisine**, backed by mountain walls and holm oak. Further south, **Cala Biriola** is marked by a limestone arch large enough to pass under by boat. Arguably the gulf's most gorgeous beach, **Cala Mariolu** is divided into two beaches by a white rocky outcrop that doubles as a popular high dive. Polished limestone pebbles meet limpid, sapphire water here. Don't leave without swimming into the cave and feeling the smooth limestone walls lapped by the current. **Cala Goloritzè** is the gulf's southernmost beach where a 140-m rock soars like a totem pole above a natural limestone arch stepping into the sea.

S'Ena 'e Thomes and Serra Orrios

Archaeology buffs should head inland from Orosei on the SS129 several kilometres past Galtellì to the *tomba di gigante* of **S'Ena 'e Thomas**. Park at the sign by the road and walk 400 m to where the 16 m by 7 m tomb rises above the overgrown vegetation. An arched central stone marks the grave's entrance; bodies were laid in the 10.9-m chamber behind.

A far more impressive Bronze Age relic is **Serra Orrios** ⓘ *T338-834 1618, daily 0900-1300 and 1400-1700, €6, €2.50 concessions*), a 10-minute drive southwest, just beyond the turnoff for Dorgali. This Nuraghic village was built between the 15th and seventh centuries BC and inhabited as late as 250 BC. There are roughly 70 well-preserved circular huts clustered around two rectangular temples; the larger and better preserved temple has been restored. A third structure has recently been found and is thought to be a sort of communal meeting place.

Grotta di Ispinigoli

ⓘ *SS125, km 32.6, T0784-963431. Mar-Jul and Sep-Nov daily 0900-1700. Aug daily 0900-1800, Dec-Feb by appointment. €7, €4.50 children.*

Fifteen kilometres south of Orosei along the SS125, you'll see a sign at km 32 for one of the world's great caves, the Grotta di Ispinigoli. Used as a shelter by goat herders until the 1970s, the cave maintains a constant 15-degree Celsius temperature (wear long sleeves).

The 45-minute tour starts at a panoramic observatory before descending 280 stairs to the base of Europe's tallest stalagmite: a single column connecting the cave's vault to its base 38 m below. Visitors then gaze down at the *L'Abisso delle Vergini* ('Abyss of the Virgins'), so-called because the Carthaginians supposedly performed a human sacrificial rite called a *molk* here, in which virgin girls were thrown down the 60-m cave to their death. Archaeologists have recovered a handful of Punic necklaces at the base of the abyss that are now displayed in Dorgali's archaeological museum.

Dorgali

Ask anyone from the Barbagie and they'll tell you the *Dorgalesi* talk like Africans. Their strikingly different dialect has led to rumours that the town was founded by Saracen pirates. Bandit blood or not, the townsfolk have evolved into a hospitable bunch with a knack for making fine handicrafts. Beneath the mountainous backdrop of Monte Bardia (882 m), **via La Marmora** and **corso Umberto** are lined with stores displaying jewellery, rugs, knives and leather accessories, not to mention Sardinia's strongest Cannonau wine from the Dorgali Cantina. The **Museo Archeologico** ① *via La Marmora, T338-834 1618, Tue-Sun 0930-1300 and 1530-1800, €3, €2 concessions*, has Neolithic pottery, a fertility stone and Punic jewellery presumably worn by the sacrificed virgins tossed down the Grotta di Ispinigoli.

Cala Gonone

East of town, a snaky road coils down Monte Bardia for 8 km to Dorgali's seaside satellite, Cala Gonone. This former fishing village got an economic boost in the 1930s, when flush Fascists began to build their art nouveau summer getaways here. The opening of the Bue Marino cave (see page 83) in the 1950s brought many other visitors in their wake and, today, the village has evolved into a lovely resort set under pine trees, where cascading geraniums dangle out of windows.

The family-friendly resort is centred around **Spiaggia Centrale**, a pebble beach next to the harbour, where kiosks offer boat rentals and excursions to the gulf's string of immaculate beaches. For more breathing room, head to the southern end of the *Lungomare* to **Spiaggia Palmasera** or continue 300 m to sheltered **Sos Dorroles**. Walkers of any level should pack a bathing suit, drive south for 3 km along viale Bue Marino until the asphalt turns to dirt, park the car at **Cala Fuili** beach around Monte Tului (916 m) and look for green signs to the impeccable **Cala Luna** cove two hours' hike away.

One of the steepest bike excursions around (or a hairpin drive) goes from Cala Gonone in the other direction, twisting up Monte Irveri (616 m), from which you have sweeping views across the gulf, and finishing at **Spiaggia Carote** (9 km) and **Spiaggia Osalla** (11 km).

Barbagia di Ollolai → *For listings, see pages 89-95.*

South of Nuoro and north of the Gennargentu National Park, the sleepy mountain towns around the Barbagia di Ollolai are a place where languid locals pass hours over card games in bars and vigorous visitors come to hike to Sardinia's highest peak: Punta La Marmora.

Ottana

The striped smoke stacks of Ottana's plastic manufacturing plant are visible for kilometres in all directions but don't let them put you off visiting the town during Carnival for its *Sos Merdules Bezzos* procession (see page 80). At other times of year it's worth popping into town to watch Franco Maritato create the horned ox masks worn in the procession (see page 94). Near Maritato's studio is the multi-coloured trachyte façade of the Romanesque **Chiesa di San Nicola**, built in 1150.

Gavoi

Gavoi's tidy stone centre nestled on a sloping mountainside makes it the most attractive town in the area. At its heart is the 15th-century **Chiesa di San Gavino**, whose towering campanile soars 30 m above a Gothic rose window. The church's square looks out over the shimmering, artificial **Lago Gusana** below, which is a favourite with fishermen and boaters. Shepherding is big business in these parts and Gavoi's economic staple is spicy *fiore sardo* pecorino cheese.

Fonni and the peaks

Watch out for grazing sheep in the middle of the road as you climb the SS389 to Sardinia's highest town, Fonni at 1000 m. This pastoral community is gradually awakening to tourism as hikers start to use its few hotels as a base camp from which to climb the Gennargentu's tallest peaks, **Brancu Spina** (1829 m) and **Punto La Marmora** (1834 m).

Follow the brown signs indicating the Brancu Spina trail 5 km south of town towards Desulo and, after ascending for 9 km, park the car and start hiking. It's a 3-km trek to the top, from where you can see north to the limestone bluffs of Corsica and south to Cagliari's harbour on clear days. Locals claim the 1½-hour onward trek from Brancu Spina to Punta La Marmora is a breeze but we recommend contacting guides in Fonni before you attempt it (see page 94).

For something easier, meander through Fonni's streets, where some of Sardinia's finest *murales* are painted along corso Carlo Alberto.

West of the Gennargentu → For listings, see pages 89-95.

Barbagia di Mandrolisai

The compact communities of the Mandrolisai lie on the western slopes of the Gennargentu and are a soothing retreat from the high temperatures and tourist hordes that characterize the Sardinian coast each summer. **Sorgono** is known for its strong Cannonau wine but is best remembered as the place that DH Lawrence condemned as a "weary village with nothing to say for itself" in *Sea and Sardinia*, before changing his mind and romanticizing about its isolated beauty. Nearby **Tonara** prides itself as the island's *torrone* (nougat) capital. Women mix honey and eggs with hazelnuts and walnuts from the Gennargentu's forests in a giant vat for up to five hours to make Torrone di Tonara, which is sold from stands at every Sardinian festival.

Aritzo

Aritzo was a favourite haunt of the Piedmontese nobility in the 19th century who came to hunt wild boar and mouflon and to escape the summer heat in its crisp climate. It remains Sardinia's most popular mountain resort. The surrounding area, the Barbagia di Belvì, is covered in dense chestnut and walnut forests, which provide material for accomplished carpenters in Aritzo and nearby Belvì.

Apart from tourism and carpentry, Aritzo's economy has long relied on a rare commodity: snow. From the 16th to the 18th centuries, workers called *niargios* would gather snow from Funtana Cungiada (1450 m), store it in straw-lined wooden freezers and then turn it into lemon sorbet. The sorbet was delivered by mule to the island's Aragonese rulers in Cagliari. Today, Aritzo's Sa Carapigna remains Sardinia's only sorbet company. The town's **Museo Etnografico** ① *via Marconi 1, T0784-629801, Tue-Sun 1030-1300 and 1630-1900, €1.60*, displays the *niargios'* old freezers and provides entry to **Sa Bovida**, a 16th-century Spanish prison.

Ogliastra → *For listings, see pages 89-95.*

Ogliastra was carved out of the southeastern corner of Nuoro in 2005 and is Italy's least populated province. Ringed by mountain ranges on three sides and plagued with poor infrastructure that has kept it isolated, this part of the island is side-stepped by visitors. It's a shame because, between the bald massifs of the Supramonte to the north, the granite Gennargentu to the west and the sharp tacchi down south, there are plenty of caves for ramblers to explore and, on the coast, fetching little Santa Maria Navarrese is Ogliastra's gateway to the Golfo di Orosei (see page 82).

Gola Gorroppu

Ogliastra begins with a bang. Of the 355-km SS125 that ploughs south from the Gallura to Cagliari, the 20-km stretch south of Dorgali is the most magnificent. The road twists through the Gennargentu National Park with views resembling an Ansel Adams photograph of sunlight dancing on the limestone walls of the Supramonte across the Flumineddu river valley. The highway climbs steadily towards the **Genna Silana** pass (1017 m) at km 183, which doubles as the starting point for the trek down to the Gola Gorroppu gorge.

If you only have time for one hike in Sardinia, set aside half a day to explore the continent's deepest ravine, often called 'Europe's Grand Canyon'. A 1½-hour trek down the rift from the pass leads to the sheer vertical walls of the **Punta Cucuttos** (888 m) and the **Punta S'Icopargiu** (1020 m) dug out of the limestone over millennia by the river Flumineddu. Continue through patches of sand and smooth rocks for another 1½ hours until you reach a series of natural pools that mark the end of the trail.

Another way to reach Gola Gorroppu is to go a few kilometres south of Dorgali on the SS125 and turn left at the brown sign indicating the site. Follow the arrows towards Gola Gorroppu on the paved road for 10 km and leave your car where the asphalt ends. Like the above approach from the Genna Silana pass, this will take you roughly six hours (including roughly two hours to ascend from the valley) and though the hike is less steep, it is also less scenic, although the drive into the valley is drop-dead gorgeous.

Regardless of your trekking ability, guides are highly recommended as they offer keen insights about the gorge's unique plants and wildlife. The best of the bunch is **Cooperativa Gorropu** (see page 94) found at the Genna Silana pass.

Baunei and the Altopiano del Golgo

Baunei looks out on to Ogliastra's coast from a natural mountain balcony. The town was founded by goat herders and is proud of its roots, which are especially in evidence on the last Sunday in August, when the town hosts the Sagra della Capra (goat festival).

On the main street opposite the Chiesa di San Nicolo, look for signs up the hill to the **Altopiano del Golgo**, a plateau at 480 m. A steep 2-km road brings you to what seems like the top of the world. Continue beyond the turn-off for **Nuraghe Coeserra** and the top-notch restaurant, **Il Golgo** (see page 92) and, after 8 km, look for a wooden sign indicating the deep limestone cave of **Su Sterru**. You can hire guides just down the road where the road loses its asphalt and scattered donkeys and pigs come into view at **Cooperativa Goloritzè** (see page 94). This *agriturismo* offers some fantastic trekking, horseback, 4x4 and boat excursions throughout the Ogliastra's lonely landscapes but you'll need to call weeks in advance as you won't get mobile phone reception on the plateau!

Santa Maria Navarrese

Ten kilometres down the hill from Baunei, Santa Maria Navarrese is a graceful seaside retreat offering similar sea-going sprees as Cala Gonone (see page 84) but on a much smaller scale. The Spanish name stems from the King of Navarra's kidnapped daughter, who was allegedly washed up on shore here after the boat on which she was hijacked got caught in a storm. Basque sailors built the whitewashed church that stands in the town's square in honour of the princess's divine protector in 1052. The massive olive tree nearby was supposedly planted the day the church was finished but, if you've already been to Luras (see page 37), this millennium-old tree will seem like a mere adolescent. For hundreds of years the rural church and its leafy counterpart were surrounded by a group of pilgrim houses occupied annually by Baunei's faithful. In the 1950s tourism started trickling in, the *cumbessiàs* came tumbling down and the present beach town sprang up.

No longer the protective stronghold of years past, the town's Aragonese watchtower now hosts occasional art exhibitions and caps the pebbly **Spiaggia Centrale**; for finer sand, head a kilometre south to Lotzorai. In warm months, Santa Maria's port offers plenty of excursions along the Golfo di Orosei: if you do nothing else in Ogliastra, book a trip with Fuori Rotta Baunei (see page 94).

Tortolì and Arbatax

Down the coast, a 3-km road lined with petrol stations, industrial zones and cheap hotels links Tortolì to its more inviting port, Arbatax. The exotic name probably stems from the Arabic word for 14 ('*arba'at 'ashar*'), since Arbatax's stout Aragonese tower was the 14th built along the coast to guard against Saracen raids. For such a small resort, Arbatax has a surprisingly well-developed tourist infrastructure: the Trenino Verde's terminus is within sight of the port, which connects the town to Civitavecchia, Genoa and Cagliari, and there's even a small airport with flights to mainland Italy. Kiosks sprinkled around the waterfront can set you up with various excursions, hotel rooms and car rentals.

The area's biggest draw are the **Rocce Rosse**, a cluster of red rocks sculpted by the wind to resemble a dribbled sand castle. It's a dramatic sight against the white sand and crystalline waters that surround it, and a tunnel drilled through its base leads to a sublime bathing spot.

Arbatax's other beaches are found behind the port, the closest being **Porto Frailis**, whose bayside setting backed by grandiose villas give it a vaguely southern California feel. The **Faro Bellavista** lighthouse perched on the beach lives up to its name with memorable views stretching along Ogliastra's coast. When Porto Frailis fills up during peak season, venture south to **San Gimignano** or the long **Orrì** beach near Tortolì.

Trenino Verde

ⓘ *Mandas to Arbatax, T070-343112, treninoverde.com. 19 Jun-11 Sep. €16.50 one way or €22 round-trip.*
Of the four Trenino Verde routes, the most scenic is undoubtedly the 160-km track from Mandas to Arbatax, which provides an excellent opportunity to explore Ogliastra's open expanses and the often overlooked **Barbagia di Seulo**. The 10-hour round-trip is best

spread out over two or more days to allow for stop-offs. Trains leave each terminus twice daily and, if you alight en route, you will have to catch the next train, seven hours later.

From Mandas, the train skirts the northern bank of **Lago Flumendosa**, before pulling in to **Sadali**. Dug deep into a gully, this 900-person hamlet is a charming place bordering one of Sardinia's largest springs. A moss-laden waterfall rushes through its centre, feeding outdoor spigots where women wash their clothes. Rangers are usually on hand as you alight from the train to escort you through the 200-m **Grotta Is Janas** (cave of the fairies) nearby, which was once a winter refuge for shepherds and their flocks. Trekkers should also alight at **Ussassai-Niala**, at the foot of the Gennargentu, and follow the path past apple trees – keeping their eyes peeled for boar, mouflon and eagles– up to a limestone ridge named **Su Casteddu 'e Joni** because of its resemblance to a castle.

Jerzu and around

West off the SS125, little Jerzu stands tall enjoying a spectacular setting under sharp limestone spires called 'tacchi' (heels). Below the town are the Cannonau vineyards which make it famous. Coming from the south, you can't miss the white tower of Jerzu's **Cantina Antichi Poderi** ① *via Umberto 1, T0782-70028, Mon-Sat 0830-1300 and 1500-1830,* which sells the town's prized wine.

The town seems to cling for dear life to the mountainous ridge with sweeping views of the Rio Pardu valley below. Other towns haven't been as lucky. Continue a few kilometres past Ulassai and signs for the 850-m **Su Marmuri grotto** ① *T0782-79707, Easter-Oct daily guided visits at 1100, 1430 and 1700,* and you'll pass the rubbled remains of **Osini Vecchio** facing **Gairo Vecchio** across the canyon (*ga* and *roa* mean 'sliding earth' in ancient Greek). In 1951, heavy rains caused the gorge's base to collapse, forcing the populations of the two towns to relocate to more secure terrain nearby.

Lanusei

Lanusei is a jumble of terracotta tiles and satellite dishes nestled into the side of a mountain. The community has adopted an air of self-importance since being crowned co-capital of the province in 2005. Racks of postcards spill out of stores, a bust of Goffredo Mameli, the composer of Italy's national anthem who lived here for a few years, stands in the central piazza, and there's even a youth hostel.

A few kilometres up the hill, the **Bosco Selene archaeological park** ① *T0782-41051, Tue-Sun 1000-1400, €4, €2 concessions,* is set in a dense oak forest at 978 m. Its crisp air, tennis courts and picnic tables make it a refreshing refuge from Lanusei. The park holds two *tombe di giganti* dating from the 15th and 14th centuries BC respectively, and archaeologists are busy uncovering **Nuraghe Genna Acilli**, which promises to be a truly unique and special Bronze Age site, unlike anything seen before.

Nuoro and Ogliastra listings

For hotel and restaurant price codes and other relevant information, see pages 11-17.

🛏 Where to stay

Nuoro and the north *p77*

€€ Grillo, *Via Monsignor Melas 14, Nuoro, T0784-38668, grillohotel.it.* Set around a straggly new development, this is Nuoro's most central hotel. The 45 rooms are far from spacious, though they are well serviced and the downstairs restaurant seems to be quite popular for lunch and dinner. Balconies cost €10 extra.

€ Casa Solotti, *Località Monte Ortobene, Nuoro, T0784-33954, casasolotti.it.* You'll pass this elegant B&B surrounded by spacious greenery on the way up the Ortobene mountain, a refreshing shift from Nuoro's clogged confusion. There are five rooms (most with balconies) overlooking vineyards. Walking trails and organized horse rides allow you to get out and about.

€ Costiolu, *10 km north of Nuoro towards Orune, T333-663 0740, agriturismocostiolu. com.* One of the oldest and most magical agriturismi in Sardinia. The Costa brothers' 160-ha farm has plenty of breathing room for three generations of dogs, cats, pigs, cows, sheep, hens, boars, goats, horses, and even a peacock. Rooms have postcard views across the farm's cork forest but with horse riding and plenty of other chances to get your hands dirty, you won't want to stay in.

€ Testone, *Località Testone, 13 km north of Nuoro towards Benetutti, T0784-230539, agriturismotestone.com.* Another family-run farm that offers everything from homemade honey, wine, bread and meats to Italian lessons! The rooms are modest, though they do have air conditioning and private baths, but the meals are lavish affairs served at long tables in a rustic dining hall.

The Supramonte *p79*

€€€€ Su Gologone, *Località Su Gologone, nr Oliena, T0784-287512, sugologone.it. Mar-Nov, Christmas and New Year only.* Central Sardinia's finest and most famous resort. From the lobby to the temporary art exhibits to the cottage-style apartments, Su Gologone is brimming with Sardinian handicrafts. The breakfast terrace and the outdoor pool (next to the spa and gym) both offer views of the Lanaittu valley. The rooms are equipped with a cushy lounge area and draped beds. If you can't stay the night, stop by for dinner at one of the island's most delectable restaurants, which serves suckling pig slow-roasted above ilex logs.

€€ CiKappa, *Corso Martin Luther King 2/4, Oliena, T0784-288024, cikappa.com.* This backpackers' lodge at the edge of town shows its age. The views across to Nuoro are appealing; the grimy showers less so, but you could do worse than eat at the hotel's restaurant. The seven rooms boast a rare commodity in the Barbagie: Wi-Fi.

Golfo di Orosei *p82*

€€€ Club Hotel Marina Beach, *Località Marina di Orosei, T0784-999900, marinabeach.it. Apr-Oct only.* This compound is the area's largest and most plush resort. The rooms are done up with traditional motifs and each has its own veranda, some overlooking the pool. A bridge leads to the resort's private beach 100 m away.

€€ Costa Dorada, *Lungomare Palmasera 45, Cala Gonone, T0784-93332, hotelcostadorada.it. Mar-Oct only.* Cala Gonone's most elegant hotel has a stone patio with five suites facing the beach 10 m away. Guests have access to the hotel's private boat to shuttle them around the Golfo di Orosei's beaches. There's a 15% supplement for stays of less than three days.

€€ Hotel Bue Marino, *Via Vespucci 8, Cala Gonone, T0784-920078, hotelbuemarino.it. Apr-Sep only.* This is one of Cala Gonone's oldest hotels but a recent makeover ensures you're in for a cushy stay overlooking the town's Spiaggia Centrale. Lounge in the rooftop hydromassage tub with views spanning the coast. Ask for a room with a sea view.

€€ S'Adde, *Via Concordia 38, Dorgali, T0784-94412, hotelsadde.it.* This central, modern hotel has a mountain feel with a wood-panelled lobby and green views. A nearby park will keep children busy, and the hotel can arrange excursions throughout the area.

€€ Su Barchile, *Via Mannu 5, Orosei, T0784-98879, subarchile.it.* This place is not for the claustrophobic! The 10 rooms are equipped with their own bath, air conditioning and TVs, but they're shoe-horned into pretty tight quarters. There's elegant (if very pricey) dining in the downstairs restaurant under a reed ceiling.

€ Codula Fuili, *Località Pranos, 3 km south of Cala Gonone, T328-734 0863, codulafuili. com.* Located near Cala Fuili beach, this small *agriturismo* has four rooms, each named after a different beach in the Golfo di Orosei. Cartoe and Oddoane have views of the sea and all have their own bathrooms. The owners will gladly let you help them tend their goats and can suggest trekking routes around the gulf.

€ Sa Corte Antica, *Via Mannu 17, Dorgali, T0784-94317, sacorteantica.it.* This B&B is found in a traditional though recently restored *Dorgalese* house tucked into a courtyard. The Pira family have given each of their three rooms a touch of class with iron bed frames and shiny-tiled bathrooms, and their hospitality is well-known in the locality.

Barbagia di Ollolai *p84*

€€ Il Pergolato, *Via Roma 10, Fonni, T0784-58455.* An attractive option located smack-bang in Fonni's centre. The few

rooms are scattered around an internal courtyard draped with grape vines. The excellent restaurant serves typical meat specialities and myrtle-flavoured sorbet.

€ Antichi Sapori, *Via Cagliari 168, Gavoi, T0784-52021, agriturismodasperanza. com.* It's a family affair inside this 18th-century farmhouse in the heart of Gavoi. Signora Todde cooks delicious meals – often including suckling pig – which are served by her and presided over by papa Above the stone dining room and hearth, two floors hold seven generous rooms with essential conveniences and private bathrooms.

West of the Gennargentu *p85*

€€ Hotel Sa Muvara, *Località Sa Muvara, Aritzo, T0784- 629336, samuvarahotel.com.* A country hotel nestled in five hectares of parkland. The rooms are generously spacious (especially the suites) with wood-panelled floors. There's a pool, gym and spa to keep you busy or staff can organize excursions in the surrounding area.

Ogliastra *p86*

€€€ Arbatasar Hotel, *Via Porto Frailis 11, Arbatax, T0782-651800, arbatasar.it.* You'll find this brand new hotel with a bright yellow exterior between the port and beaches. The rooms come with modern comforts in breezy colours. If the five-minute walk to the beach is too far, there's a pool out back.

€€ Hotel Agugliastra, *Piazza Principessa di Navarra, Santa Maria Navarrese, T0782-615005, hotelagugliastra.it.* The plain white hallways and rooms are reminiscent of a hospital ward but the beds are comfortable and the bathrooms are spacious. The hotel's terrace café is a popular spot, so on summer nights you may need to use earplugs.

€€ Hotel Nicoletta, *Via Lungomare, Santa Maria Navarrese, T0782-614045, hotelnicoletta.info. Mar-Nov only.* The more upscale of Santa Maria's two central hotels, this squat rust-coloured villa is surrounded by flower beds and has 28 rooms. Some have balconies overlooking the main drag, and all have modern comforts.

€€ La Bitta, *Località Porto Frailis, Arbatax, T0782-667080, hotellabitta.it. Closed Jan.* Arbatax's most graceful hotel is a few steps off the beach at Porto Frailis. Rooms come with arching ceilings, Roman-style columns and massages on your balcony.

€ Da Concetta, *Corso Umberto I 111, Jerzu, T0782 70197, hotelristorantedaconcetta. it.* This is about the only choice in town. Luckily, the elderly Concetta is beyond hospitable and has several charming rooms on offer, with air-conditioning and private baths. Guests have access to the rooftop terrace with views across the valley. When hunger calls, walk across the street to find Concetta making homemade *culurgiones* (dumplings). She can also set up trekking excursions around Jerzu's limestone *tacchi*.

€ La Nuova Luna, *Via Indipendenza 35, Lanusei, T0782-41051, lanuovaluna.it.* Why a youth hostel sprang up in Lanusei remains a mystery but there's no denying its charm. The large stone dining room and wood-panelled ceiling resemble a cosy lodge, and €18 for a bed in a three-to-seven-person dormitory is a steal… especially considering you'll probably have the place to yourself.

Campsites

Camping Telis, *Località Porto Frailis, Arbatax, T0782-667140, campingtelis.com.* A few steps away from Hotel La Bitta, this year-round campsite boasts its own private beach with free lounge chairs for its bungalow and mobile home guests. There's also a small playground, tennis court and a dive centre on site.

🍴 Restaurants

Nuoro and the north *p77*

€€€ Canne al Vento, *Via Biasi, Nuoro, T0784-201762. Mon-Sat 1930-2300.* Named after Grazia Deledda's famous novel, this restaurant on the outskirts of town fittingly serves up classic Sardinian fare, from *prosciutto* antipasto to pecorino and honey dessert, and everything in between.

€€€ Ciusam, *Viale Ciusa 55, Nuoro, T0784-257052. Wed-Mon 1930-2330.* Nuoro's best pizzas are heated inside Ciusa's wood-burning ovens. For something heavier, try the risotto with Cannonau wine and pecorino cheese.

€€ Da Giovanni, *Via IV Novembre 9, Nuoro, T0784-30562. Mon-Sat 1230-1430 and 2000-2200.* It's a bit hard to find, but the wild boar served here since the 1950s is worth the effort. Try it atop *gnochetti* or *fettucine* noodles, or go with the *filindreu* mutton broth made famous by Lula's bandits.

Cafés and bars

Caffè America, *Piazza Italia 5, Nuoro. Daily 0700-2200.* This elegant wooden haunt is a popular spot with locals and is conveniently close to the tourist office. There are lots of yummy salads and plenty of wines available by the glass.

Pit Stop, *Via Brofferio 19, Nuoro, T0784-257030. Mon-Sat 2000-2400.* Aside from corso Garibaldi's cafés, this is Nuoro's only other drinking spot. Cheap prices draw a younger crowd.

Plada Caffè, *Corso Garibaldi 141, Nuoro, T0784-238873. Daily 0630-2130.* Offers good panini and people-watching.

The Supramonte *p79*

€€€ Masiloghi, *Via Galiani 68, Oliena, T0784-285696. Apr-Oct daily 1230-1430 and 1930-2245.* Choose from four fixed menus or select à la carte specialities. The fare, like the decor, is decidedly Sardinian; you can't go wrong with young boar in a fennel sauce or *gnochetti* noodles. The restaurant also runs a B&B.

€€ 'Sa Rosada, *Piazza Europa 2, Mamoiada, T0784-56713. Wed-Mon 1230-1430 and 1930-2200.* A fetching little place tucked into a veranda with an all-Sardo menu that changes daily.

Golfo di Orosei *p82*

€€€€ Il Pescatore, *Via Acqua Dolce 7, Cala Gonone, T0784-93174. Easter-Oct daily 1215-1500 and 1900-2230.* Fish is the main melody in this oversized upper-crust establishment. Three women serve *burrida dorgalese* soup and fish any way you want it, caught by their brother. If Vermintino wine from Gallura doesn't find its way into your glass, you'll probably taste it in chef Patrizia's sauces.

€€€ Colibrì, *Via Floris 7, Dorgali, T0784-96054. Mid Mar-mid Nov Mon-Sat 1230-1430 and 2000-2230.* This seasonal restaurant has been a mainstay for nearly 30 years, serving typical local *pane frattau* (Sardinian 'lasagne' made with pecorino and *pane carasau*, topped with an egg), goat, lamb and wild boar.

€€€ La Taverna, *Piazza Marconi 6, Orosei, T0784-998330. Mon-Sat 1300-1530 and 1900-2100.* Sit outside surrounded by cactus and flowers or inside where farm tools are stuck to the wall. The wild boar is popular, as are the *maccarose de busa* pasta and the blackberry sorbet.

€€€ Sant'Elene, *Località Sant'Elene, Dorgali, T0784-94572. Apr-Sep daily 1300-1430 and 2000-2200, Oct-Mar by request.* Two kilometres north of Dorgali on the SS125, this hotel-restaurant combo offers a nice mix of surf and turf. The owners produce their own vegetables, olive oil, tagliatelle and wine.

€€ Aquarius, *Lungomare Palmasera 34, Cala Gonone, T0784-93428. Apr-Oct daily 1200-1500 and 1900-2300.* A family-run restaurant near the beach serving seafood, meat and pizzas. The *aragosta alla catalana* comes recommended, and head chef Sebastiano Mula will round-up shellfish from local fishermen if you call ahead.

€€ Da Diego, *Piazza Sant'Antonio 22, Orosei, T0784-998072. Tue-Sun 1230-1500 and 1930-2300.* Orosei's best pizzeria has a laid-back setting. Spaghetti with *bottarga* and plenty of meats are also on hand, as is Oliena's famous Nepente wine.

Cafés and bars

Yesterday Caffè, *Via Nazionale 48, Orosei. Mon-Sat 0830-1230 and 1630-2400.* A few bits of Beatles memorabilia are hung inside but the outdoor seating on the cobblestones behind the main street is more inviting. Come here for coffee by day and cocktails at night.

Barbagia di Ollolai *p84*

€€€ Santa Rughe, *Via Carlo Felice 2, Gavoi, T0784-53774. May-Aug daily 1900-2200, Sep-Apr Thu-Tue 1900-2200.* This cosy retreat serves pizzas and more hearty fare. In spring, try the traditional *erbudzu* soup filled with wild herbs.

€€€ Su Ninnieri, *Località Bruncu Spina, Fonni, T0784-57729. Wed-Mon 1900-2300.* Drive towards Desulo to the junction for Brancu Spina and follow the signs to this country joint. Rustic recipes abound here.

West of the Gennargentu *p85*

€€€€ Su Muvara, *Località Fontana Rubia, Aritzo, T0784-629336. May-Oct daily 1900-2200.* This restaurant is attached to a hotel of the same name and enjoys views of mountains and trees from its terrace. The porcini mushrooms and homemade torrone dessert are good.

€€ Moderno, *Viale Kennedy 6, Aritzo, T0784-629229. Easter-Oct daily 1300-1500 and 2015-2200.* There's nothing 'moderno' about this haunt; it was one of the area's first hotels. Downstairs, Signora Manca whips up homemade pasta dishes.

Ogliastra *p86*

€€€ Da Lenin, *Via San Gemiliano 19, Tortolì, T0782-624422. Mon-Sat 1930-2245.* It's a good thing the dilapidated façade of this joint doesn't reflect the food. Seafood is king at Lenin Mura's restaurant. Locals recommend the shrimp with ragù and the fresh lobster.

€€€ Il Golgo, *Località Golgo, via Bitzocoro 10, Baunei, T0782-610732. Apr-Sep daily 1230-1430 and 1930-2245.* Perched on the

Altopiano di Golgo in a typical stone hut with a wooden roof, the restaurant offers wonderful meat dishes.

€€€ Ristorante Lungomare, *Via Turru 10, Santa Maria Navarrese, T0782-614041, Wed-Mon 1230-1400 and 1930-2200.* Locals rate Lungomare's seafood as the best in a town with few options. Spaghetti with clams is passable; sea bass stuffed with shrimp is better. The restaurant's rooms overlook the port below.

€€ Lo Spiedo d'Ogliastra, *Via Zinnias 23, Tortolì, T0782-623856. Daily 1230-1500 and 1930-2300.* A restaurant/pizzeria run by the Scattu family. The *culurgiones* dumplings are yummy.

Cafés and bars
L'Olivastro, *Via Lungomare, Santa Maria Navarrese, T0782-615513. May-mid Oct daily 0730-0200.* A mellow drinking and mingling spot. Choose from beer, cocktails and panini.

🎭 Entertainment

Nuoro and Ogliastra *p75*
Clubs
Il Gazebo, *500 m south of Santa Maria Navarrese towards Lotzorai, Ogliastra, T0782-669581. Jun-mid Sep.* Ravers come from all around the coast to dance the night away at this club, which is loved by hormone-driven males and hated by the sleep-deprived folk at the two campsites next door. Hours and entrance fees vary.
Lo Skrittiore, *Località Iscrittiore, Cala Gonone, Golfo di Orosei, T339-330 3708. May-Sep Fri-Sun 2300-0300.* A few kilometres up the hill toward Dorgali is this popular disco that blasts everything from reggae to revival. Check the kiosks at the port for dates.
Toma Alternative Bar, *Porto Santa Maria Navarrese, Ogliastra. May-Sep daily 2130-0300.* Live music permeates from this two-storey wooden bar with romantic views overlooking the port. The inside has a modish Middle-Eastern theme.

☺ Festivals and events

Nuoro and Ogliastra *p75*
The most important and unique celebrations in the Barbagie take place for the **Festa di Sant'Antonio Abate** in January and for **Carnevale** in February (see page 18), with the most notable processions in Mamoiada and Ottana (see page 80), Orosei, Dorgali and Gavoi. Other calendar highlights include the **S'Incontru** Easter parade in Oliena and the **Festa dell'Assunta** on 15 August in Orgosolo. Two days later, Orgosolo hosts a Palio-style horse race that attracts jockeys from throughout Sardinia. This region also has numerous harvest and food festivals. Tonara celebrates its famous nougat on Easter Monday in the **Sagra del Torrone**, with plenty of samples, while Jerzu hosts the boozy **Sagra del Vino** in August, honouring the town's Cannonau wine. Aritzo showcases its sorbet at the **Festa di San Carapigna** and marks the chestnut and hazelnut harvest with the **Sagra delle Castagne e delle Nocciole** in October.

🛍 Shopping

The Supramonte *p79*
Maschere Mameli, *Corso Vittorio Emanuele III 7, Mamoiada, T0784-56222. Mon-Sat 0900-1230 and 1630-1900.* Ruggero Mameli is Mamoiada's leading mask maker and his workshop is a great place to buy the town's trademark souvenir.
Prodotti Tipici Sardi, *Piazza Santa Maria 14, Oliena, T0784-288110. Wed-Mon 0830-1300 and 1700-2000, Tue 0830-1300.* Local cheeses and meats, and Oliena's famous Nepente wine.

Golfo di Orosei *p82*
Arte Sarda, *Via Nazionale, Orosei, T346-700 0694. May-Sep daily 0900-1300 and 1630-2000, Oct-Apr closed Sun.* The best stocked of three neighbouring souvenir shops, with a good selection of hand-woven baskets.

EnoDelizie, *Via Lamarmora 149, Dorgali, T0784-96633. Mon-Sat 0900-1300 and 1630-2000.* A great place to pick up Dorgali's famously strong Cannonau wine, as well as leading brands from throughout Sardinia.

Barbagia di Ollolai *p84*
Maschere Tradizionali Ottanesi, *Piazza Sant'Antonio, Ottana, T328-652 0069. Daily 0800-1300 and 1400-2000.* Franco Maritato is the man behind Ottana's bizarre Carnival masks (see page 80). His horned and snouted designs run from €35 to €130.
Sos Zillonarzos, *Via Roma 227, Gavoi, T349-198 2731. Mon-Sat 0730-1200 and 1630-2030.* A family-run operation, selling homemade breads and desserts, meat and lots of Gavoi's *fiore sardo* pecorino cheese.

☉ What to do

Golfo di Orosei *p82*
See also **Fuori Rotta Baunei**, below.
Cooperative Ghivine, *Via Lamarmora 69, Dorgali, T349-442 5552, ghivine.com.* Dorgali's leading outdoor specialist leads daily summer excursions up to the Supramonte, around the Golfo di Orosei, through Ogliastra's *tacchi* and into a variety of archaeological sites.
L'Argonauta, *Via dei Lecci 10, Cala Gonone, T0784-93046, argonauta.it. Apr-Oct only.* Choose from 30 dives through the underwater cliffs or sunken Second World War ships scattered around the Golfo di Orosei. The guides are a friendly, English-speaking bunch who also run a few area treks and can suggest lodging options. Orosei Diving Center, *Località Marina di Orosei, T349-598 3533, oroseidivingcenter. it.* Explore several sunken ships and red coral reefs around Orosei with this young, energetic, English-speaking dive team. Courses are available for both adults and children.

Barbagia di Ollolai *p84*
Barbagia No Limits, *Via Cagliari 85, Gavoi, T0784-529016, barbagianolimits.it.* This adventure operator offers canyoning, canoeing, trekking and week-long camping trips into the Barbagie's hinterland.
Gennargentu Escursioni, *Via Porrino 15/B, Fonni, T0784-589038, gennargentuescursioni. it.* Arrange for an English-speaking guide to lead you on various trekking excursions throughout the Gennargentu and Supramonte mountain ranges lasting from one to three days.

Ogliastra *p86*
Cooperative Goloritzè, *Località Golgo, Baunei, T0782-610599, coopgoloritze.com.* This is one of Sardinia's most established excursion companies, offering one- to three-day jaunts on horseback, 4x4 or boat from Tiscali to the Golfo di Orosei with English-speaking guides. Their lodge serves appetizing dishes and is a wonderful place to make camp for a few days.
Cooperative Gorropu, *Via Sa Preda Lada 2, Urzulei, T333-850 7157, gorropu.com.* If you want to explore Gola Gorroppu, put your faith in Sandra, an upbeat German expat who knows the canyon like the back of her hand. She and her husband, an Urzulei local, also lead other trips around central Sardinia.
Fuori Rotta Baunei, *Marina di Santa Maria Navarrese, T339-838 7788, fuorirottabaunei. it.* This class act can't be recommended highly enough. Cruise the Golfo di Orosei aboard a converted fishing vessel that holds a maximum of 15 people, remodelled by Captain Antonello himself. Antonello speaks functional English and leads informative and interesting tours of the gulf's beaches, gladly accommodating any preferences to go to one beach over another. Sign up for the three-course lunch on board: the fresh seafood salad and shrimp pasta are outstanding!

⊖ Transport

Nuoro *p77*

The parts of Nuoro town worth exploring are compact enough to traverse on foot. If you have a car, park in the higher part of town, as it's a steep climb from the newer development (where the ARST bus station is located) to the centre. Bus 8 runs frequently from the bus station up to Monte Ortobene.

Bus station: **Autolinee ARST**, viale Sardegna, T0784 295030 (daily 0600-2000). Two ARST buses run daily from Nuoro to Olbia (2 hrs 30 mins/3 hrs) and to Cagliari (2 hrs 30 mins/5 hrs). There are fairly frequent daily buses between Nuoro and Mamoiada (20 mins), Ottana (30 mins), Gavoi (1 hr 10 mins) and Fonni (40 mins-1 hr 30 mins), plus four buses to Orosei (50 mins), one to Tortolì (2 hrs 40 mins) and one to Aritzo (1 hr 55 mins).

Train station: **Stazione delle FS**, via Lamarmora 10, T0784-30115. There are regular trains between Nuoro and Macomer (1 hr), where you can connect to Cagliari and Sassari.

Ogliastra *p86*

From Tortolì one daily ARST bus travels to Nuoro (2 hrs 40 mins) and five to Cagliari (2 hrs 45 mins). See page 87 for information on the Trenino Verde to Arbatax.

① Directory

Nuoro *p77*

Money ATMS: corso Garibaldi. **Medical services Ospedale Civile**, via Mannironi, T0784-240237. **Farmacia Gali**, corso Garibaldi 65, T0784-30143. **Post office Poste Italiane**, piazza Crispi 8, T0784-30554 (Mon-Fri 0815-1840, Sat 0900-1300). **Tourist information** piazza Italia 19, T0784-30083 (Mon-Sat 0900-1300 and 1600-1900).

Contents

Background

History

Sardinia's strategic position at the crossroads of the Mediterranean sealed its fate as a pawn in the messy tug-of-war between Middle Eastern, African and European powers. As a result, the island has endured 1500 years of raids, rule and regulation by more than a dozen foreign occupiers. Yet, Sardinia's most distinctive characteristics didn't evolve under Punic, Roman or Spanish rule, but emerged long before anyone else was looking, when the Sardi were left to their own, independent devices.

Neolithic Sardinia

Primitive flint and quartz tools from as far back as 450,000 BC found near Perfugas attest to the presence of humans in Sardinia from the Paleolithic age, but Sardinia's past doesn't come into focus until the Neolithic age (6000-3500 BC). This prehistoric renaissance saw humans develop pottery, move from caves into outdoor settlements, and shift from hunter-gatherer subsistence lifestyles to agricultural and livestock farming. Of the world's Neolithic peoples, those in Sardinia were likely to be as wealthy as any thanks to the island's deposits of obsidian. This rare volcanic glass could be shaped into arrowheads, knives and other tools, rendering it more valuable than gold in the Neolithic world. From its discovery at Monte Arci in the eighth millennium BC, mined obsidian became prehistoric Sardinia's most important economic resource and was traded as far away as Tuscany and France.

As early Sardinians came into contact with the outside world, they exchanged not only goods, but also artistic techniques and religious theories, paving the way for the development of the Bonu Ighinu culture (4000-3500 BC). This period saw the production of the first stone statues of the chubby female Mother Goddess representing fertility, which became an icon of the island's earliest known religion. The Bonu Ighinu was a relatively peaceful matriarchal society, with women running domestic and village affairs while men often worked away in the fields.

Sardinia's Neolithic ingenuity peaked with the so-called Ozieri Culture (3500-2700 BC), named after artefacts retrieved from the San Michele cave near present-day Ozieri. Sardinians started burying the dead in *domus de janas* ('fairy houses'), rock-cut tombs, ranging from single chambers to elaborate necropoli. Elongated stone menhirs were placed near burial sites to correspond to astrological cycles, and artists created pottery festooned with spirals and human figurines. The apotheosis of Ozieri engineering was the raised cult temple at Monte d'Accodi, resembling nothing less than a Mesopotamian ziggurat pyramid.

The dawn of the Chalcolithic (or Copper) Age marked a distinct turning point in early Sardinia. Ozieri's craftsmen and their descendants were some of the earliest in the Mediterranean to develop metal tools, effectively marking the end of the peaceful farming society and the birth of competitive, warrior-driven clans. Artists began depicting menhirs as either female, with protruding breasts, or male, wielding a carved, double-edged dagger. The dominance of the male menhirs, coupled with the disappearance of the chubby female goddess statues, seems to suggest that, although Neolithic Sardinia may have developed as a matriarchal society, metals gave it a serious injection of testosterone. As social tensions rose with the Chalcolithic arms race, turreted walls were erected to defend villages and the first proto-nuraghi were developed. These were raised, rectangular stone platforms with galleries and staircases, topped by a wooden hut: the precursor to the great Nuraghic towers that were to come.

Nuraghic Sardinia and the Bronze Age

Most scholars identify the Nuraghic age (beginning 1800 BC) as the defining period in Sardinia's history, as individualized cultures developed into a distinct island-wide society characterized by architectural unity. In the absence of any evidence of a Nuraghic written language, historians have studied the thousands of visual clues that dot the island's landscape to shed light on a Bronze Age society that is finally gaining recognition as one of the Mediterranean's most advanced.

The Nuraghic period gets its name from its most identifiable monuments: stone towers known as a nuraghi. Built between 1600 and 1000 BC, over 7,000 of these truncated, cone-shaped monuments remain, with countless others cannibalized over the years. Though they bear a resemblance to the underground tombs constructed by Sardinians' trading partners, the Mycenaeans, radiocarbon dating and archaeological evidence suggest that the construction and engineering ingenuity of these structures came from the Sardi themselves.

The earlier single-tower nuraghi were likely territorial markers between clans from which another nuraghe could almost always be seen, forming a communication chain. Between 1500 and 1200 BC, many mono-tower nuraghi developed into Bronze Age castles, rising up to 27 m and sprouting as many as 17 towers, as at Nuraghe Arrubiu. These were likely palaces for a tribal chief, complete with connecting bastions, escape routes and courtyards designed to defend village settlements that increasingly sought their protection (Nuraghe Su Nuraxi is one of the best examples).

Nuraghic inhabitants enjoyed a surprisingly enlightened social structure. People lived in huts with circular, stone bases and thatched roofs, similar to the *pinnettas* still used by Sardinia's present-day shepherds. There were warriors, farmers, shepherds and artists, all of whom contributed to the building of nuraghi and paid a tax of grain or animal meat to the chief, which was distributed among the entire community. At the time of death (around 35 years' old) people were buried in vast communal *tombe di giganti* (giants' tombs). The number of women and children found inside suggests an indiscriminate burial practice regardless of social hierarchy.

By 1200 BC local craftsmen were beginning to manufacture bronze objects, which would later evolve into intricate *bronzetti*. These miniature statues were left as votive offerings at well temples as an integral part of Nuraghic religious practice and provide a window to the social strata that comprised the Nuraghic population, showing warriors, chiefs, hunters, wrestlers, women, animals, and imaginary beings.

Bronzetti production coincided with the decline of nuraghe building and the dawn of a new political and social structure. Many nuraghi were dismantled and incorporated into villages, and the community-orientated structures overseen by tribal chiefs were replaced by conclaves of landowners who nominated political representatives. More significantly, foreign merchants were tired of long-distance trading with the Sardi and were anxious to establish settlements on the island. Nuraghic villages coexisted for a time beside their new neighbours during the early Iron Age (900-750 BC), but the once-formidable island-wide society was on its last legs when the Punic invaders came knocking.

Phoenicians, Carthaginians and Romans

In about 1000 BC, Phoenician merchants began snooping around Sardinia's southwestern coasts, using the island's placid inlets to rest or repair their ships along their well-established trade route between present-day Lebanon and Spain. Lured by Sardinia's rich mineral deposits, these temporary moorings led to established settlements at Nora, Karalis (Cagliari), Sulci (Sant'Antioco), Bithia (Chia) and Tharros between the ninth and seventh centuries BC.

The Phoenicians arrival in Sardinia was largely peaceful, as the incomers generally remained on the coasts and integrated little with the inland inhabitants. However, they did import Etruscan and Greek pottery to the island and introduced Sardinia to urban design and writing: the defining characteristics of a unified civilisation that were never achieved by Nuraghic rival clans.

The happy coexistence turned sour in the seventh to sixth centuries BC, when the Phoenicians began expanding their settlements into Sardinia's interior, pushing indigenous villagers off their land and leading Nuraghic tribes to raid the Phoenicians' inland mining base at Monte Sirai. Fearful of a unified island uprising, the Phoenicians enlisted their powerful African colony, Carthage (present-day Tunisia), to help subdue the Sardi.

Sardinian tribes fought valiantly against their Punic invaders. Utilizing the maze-like corridors of nuraghi to conduct guerilla assaults, the Sardi humiliated Malchus – who had previously defeated the Greeks and conquered most of Sicily in a matter of months – sending his troops packing in 540 BC. However, not before the invaders had introduced the malaria-carrying mosquitoes that would ravage Sardinia for the next 1,500 years.

It took another 30 years for Punic forces to take control of the island, with the exception of its forbidding mountainous interior. The Carthaginians expanded Phoenician settlements into profitable maritime cities and exploited Sardinia's agro-pastoral land and mines, enslaving much of the indigenous population while privatizing the island's natural resources. Local magistrates called *sufetes* governed cities and, for the first time, the island existed as part of a larger colony. Having stripped the Nuraghic culture of its ports, pastures and political influence, Carthage seemed poised to reign as the western Mediterranean's dominating force, until Rome flexed its muscles.

The First Punic War (264-241 BC) saw Rome sack Carthage's formidable navy, forcing it to surrender Sicily and agree to a strict peace treaty. To add insult to injury, many Punic soldiers returned to Sardinia to discover that their depleted empire could no longer afford to pay them! Outraged, they revolted and pulled the ultimate about-face: they appealed to Rome. Recognizing a chaotic situation, the Romans violated their peace treaty in 238 BC and seized Sardinia's principal Punic cities without resistance. By 227 BC, a Roman governor controlled Sardinia and Corsica as Rome's second province.

Though they might not have realized it, the Romans had entered a very unstable situation in Sardinia. After 271 years of Carthaginian rule, much of the island was completely absorbed in Punic culture, and the remaining unruly *Sardi Pelliti* (hairy Sardinians), as the Romans called them, of the mountainous interior were not exactly known for rolling out the red carpet for outsiders. In 215 BC, during the Second Punic War (218-201 BC), Punic-Sardinian forces aligned under a Sardinian leader, Ampsicora, to revolt against the Roman occupiers in the name of *Bellum Sardum*. It took a fleet of 50 Roman ships to quell the insurgents but worse was yet to come. In 177 BC, Rome sent 30,000 soldiers and 5,200 horsemen to suppress indigenous uprisings around the Gennargentu mountains, killing 12,000 Sardi and enslaving or imprisoning another 80,000. Despite the slaughter, the Romans endured another 15 rebellions from the Gennargentu without ever fully subduing these mountain-dwelling mavericks. The Romans dubbed the area 'Barbarie' (present-day Barbagie) after the barbarian-like ferocity of its inhabitants.

Elsewhere, the Romans did much to modernize Sardinian infrastructure and laid the foundations for much of Sardinia's subsequent cultural development. Aside from the typical civic projects that accompany Roman *municipia* (theatres, forums, baths, temples, etc), they introduced Latin (from which Sardinia's native language, Sardo, derives), increased agriculture and mining production, spread Christianity and built a road network from Cagliari to Porto Torres that paved the way for today's SS131.

Vandals, Byzantines, Arabs and giudicati

The collapse of Rome created a power vacuum in Sardinia and the island's advantageous geographic position attracted numerous unwanted guests.

First came the Vandals, Germanic warriors who launched attacks on Sardinia from their colony in North Africa, occupying the island in AD 456. However, the scant records available from this period suggest that the Vandals' grip on the island was limited to a few coastal areas.

By 534, a reinvigorated Roman Empire based in Constantinople (Byzantium) was eager to reconquer the western half of its former glory. Led by Emperor Justinian, the Byzantines slashed their way through the Italian mainland before defeating the Vandals in North Africa. Following an island-wide insurrection in 533, Sardinia became one of Byzantium's seven African provinces.

The Byzantines ruled Sardinia for over 300 years. They built the island's first churches and established an advanced political structure that endured, in one way or another, throughout the Middle Ages. A military commander called a '*dux*' was in charge of keeping an eye on the unyielding rebels from the Barbagie, and the island was divided into four provinces, each ruled by a judge called a *judex provinciae*. The districts were further divided into *partes* (counties) overseen by a *curatore* (representative), with individual villages led by a *maiore* (mayor).

By the eighth century, Arab and Berber armies had succeeded in conquering much of Northern Africa and began pushing their way into Sardinia and Spain, posing a real threat to the Byzantine Empire. With its resources stretched thin, Constantinople seemed unable and unwilling to defend its distant colony. In 705 Arab raiders sailed away with 3,000 Sardi as prisoners. They even briefly occupied Karalis (Cagliari), threatening to conquer the island in 752.

While sporadic Arabic raids would be on the menu in Sardinia for the next 1000 years, the absence of sustained outside intervention permitted a nascent Sardinian independence to take shape. From the eighth century, the *judexes* created by the Byzantines gradually evolved into Sardinian-controlled *giudicati* (sovereign states or kingdoms) run by an elected *giudice*. The four *giudicati* were officially partitioned in 856: Torres, the most politically active, to the northwest; Arborea, the most unified, around Oristano; Gallura, the smallest, poorest, and most isolated, in the northeast; and Cagliari, the largest, wealthiest and most violent, in the south.

In 1015 the Arab emirate Mujahid launched a sea attack against the island, forcing the four *giudicati* to appeal to Pope Benedict VIII for assistance. Rival naval powers Genoa and

Pisa intervened and the unified forces rid the island of its Arab invaders but this left the Sardi with another problem: their new allies had no intention of leaving.

Pisa and Genoa, Aragon and Spain

By the 11th century, the four *giudicati* had developed into independent states, each frequently clashing with its neighbours in a continuing tug-of-war over land, wealth and power. Recognizing the economic opportunity offered by the island's political instability, the Pisans and Genoese established alliances with Sardinia's rival factions, which shifted with the winds for the next 300 years.

On the surface, the *giudicati* seemed to have entered into a healthy marriage with their mainland *maestri*: the Pisans and Genoese generated a period of island-wide progress, bringing with them the modern trappings of medieval Europe. International trade boomed, irrigation techniques improved, and salt and mining extraction increased. Sardinia's strengthened international alliances also enticed monastic orders to the island from Provence and Pisa to spread Christianity and work with local artists to create a series of stunning Romanesque churches. But Pisa and Genoa had not come to make friends and, as their involvement in the island's internal affairs increased, so did their control of its economy and government.

By the 12th century the *giudicati* had begun ceding large swathes of land to Pisa and Genoa's noble families: Malaspina in Bosa, della Gherardesca in the Iglesiente, Doria in Sassari, and Visconti throughout the island. In calculated moves, these wealthy barons began marrying their way into power and, after 1250, three of the *giudicati* passed into Pisan or Genoese control, leaving only Arborea to carry the torch of Sardinian independence.

While Italian powers were fast dividing up Sardinia for themselves, bigger sharks began circling the Mediterranean. After snatching power from Charles of Anjou and his Sicilian territories in 1282, the Barcelona-based Aragonese seemed poised for a full-scale invasion. Anxious to maintain his ecclesial sway in Sicily, Pope Bonifacio VIII created the 'Kingdom of Sardinia and Corsica' and offered it to the King Jaume II of Aragon in 1297 in lieu of Sicily. As a competing maritime power of both Genoa and Pisa, Jaume was all too eager to accept the Pope's open invitation to invade.

After establishing an alliance with their Genoese rivals, the Aragonese finally made good on Bonifacio's offer in 1323 and sent 11,000 troops to Sardinia. Aligned with independent Arborea and with the Genoese Malaspina and Doria families, the Catalan-Aragonese forces quickly took control of Iglesias, Cagliari and the rest of Pisa's holdings. However, Arborea soon realized that the Aragonese were only using them as a pawn to gain control of the island and rebelled against their former allies in a series of revolts beginning in 1353.

The fight for the independent *Repubblica Sardistica* was championed by Arborea's Mariano IV. Known as Sardinia's greatest *giudice*, Mariano crushed an Aragonese insurgence in Oristano in 1368. Better remembered, however, is Mariano's daughter, Eleonora d'Arborea, who became *giudicessa* in 1383 and created the *Carta de Logu*, an exhaustive 198-chapter code of progressive laws written in Sardo and including concepts such as female suffrage, joint property ownership, the liberty to divorce following sexual assault, and the recognition of servants as citizens, a first in Italy. Amended only slightly over the years, the Carta formed the legal core of a nascent Sardinian nation and remained the law of the island until 1817.

Sardinia's struggle for independence started to unravel following Eleonora's untimely death in 1404. In the Battle of Sanluri in 1409 half of the island's volunteer army of

20,000 men were killed by the Aragonese, leading to a last-stand revolt in the Battle of Macomer in 1478.

After more than 100 years of struggle with their subjects, the Aragonese were ready to wring what reward they could from Sardinia. Their rule was marked by feudalism and taxes designed to fund the Iberians' expansionist dreams. Sardinia's new landlords did their best to ethnically cleanse the island by replacing Sardo with Catalan as the official language and banishing the indigenous inhabitants from their fortified settlements.

The marriage of Isabella and Ferdinand in 1476 brought Spain's confederation of states into a unified monarchy and did little to help Sardinia's cause. While many Cagliritani merchants and artists benefited from the profitable Spanish trade, political opponents were imprisoned and tortured, and elsewhere on the island, the neglected coast suffered from malaria outbreaks and Arab raids. As their empire declined in the 16th and 17th centuries, the Spaniards constructed hundreds of pirate watchtowers along the Sardinian shoreline but could rarely be bothered to come to the island's aid.

Austrians, Savoyards and Italian Unification

When the last Spanish Hapsburg, Charles II, died in 1700 without heirs, the Spanish Empire died along with him, leaving Sardinia for the taking once again. Like much of Europe, Sardinia divided its loyalties between Spain's two competing successors, the French and the Austrians, until an Austrian-British alliance disembarked in Cagliari in 1708. Expanding their grip over much of Sardinia, the Austrians thwarted two French invasions until the Treaty of Utrecht officially placed the island under the control of the Austrio-Hungarian Empire in 1713.

Austrian rule over Sardinia lasted all of five years, after which it was passed to the growing independent state of Savoy based in Turin. The Dukes of Savoy were a power-hungry bunch who lacked a crown. Eager to claim a kingdom, they revitalized Pope Bonifacio VIII's long-forgotten Kingdom of Sardinia and sent a series of viceroys to rule in Cagliari. However, the Savoyards ultimately showed as little interest in their new kingdom as previous rulers, and Sardinia remained a neglected and impoverished colony.

The French Revolution brought more trouble. Lacking any Savoyard support, the Sardinians were forced to field a militia and fight off French attacks. In 1793, Sardinian forces succeeded in repelling a young Napoleon Bonaparte from the Maddalena islands. Following their heroic stand, Sardinians sought the same autonomous rights their neighbours enjoyed in Corsica but the Savoyard King Vittorio Amedeo III refused the request for constitutional reform, causing fiery uprisings to erupt throughout the island from 1794 to 1796, killing several royal administrators.

In the 19th century, two Savoyard kings finally showed more interest in the island: Carlo Felice (Happy Charlie: 1821-1831) built Sardinia's modern Cagliari–Porto Torres SS131 highway, and his successor, Carlo Alberto, sought to abolish Sardinia'a crippling feudalism in the 1830s and '40s. However, the existing Enclosure Act of 1823 privatized public land once harvested by Sardinia's peasants and economic reforms resulted in heavy taxation. In Sardinia's poorest regions, frustration often led to banditry. In 1847, Carlo Alberto merged the Kingdom of Sardinia with Piedmont, which gave Piedmontese lumberjacks a green light to deforest much of Sardinia for their own gain.

Despite its impoverished status, Sardinia played a central role in Italian unification in 1861. The island not only hosted the leader of the Risorgimento, Giuseppe Garibaldi who built his home on Caprera, but also provided Italy's first king, Carlo Emanuele, when

Saying no to NATO

Sardinia's position at the crossroads of two continents has long been coveted for military means. While tourists are lured by postcard images of sweeping valleys and lonely shores, NATO has recognized that the island's lack of development makes it a perfect location for testing weapons. Today, Sardinia has 23 military bases, which occupy more land per square kilometre of the country than anywhere else in the world, and they are found in the most unlikely of places, including La Maddalena national park.

While the military's presence contributes over $40 million annually to Sardinia's economy through jobs and construction contracts, many Sardinians feel that these bases are the latest chapter in the island's history of outside control. It's a stormy subject on a sunny island and one that recently came to a head.

The US has had a NATO nuclear submarine base on the island of Santo Stefano since 1972. In 2003, an atomic submarine from the base hit a reef in the Strait of Bonifacio and, although no radioactive waste was leaked, this near catastrophic event, which was kept secret for days, outraged local residents and triggered Sardinia's then-regional president, Renato Soru, to strive to remove all US military bases from Sardinia.

Sardinia is effectively powerless to intervene in the national treaties that regulate the military bases, but Soru's campaign to transform these garrisons into resorts didn't go unnoticed and in February 2008 the US ceased its military operations here. While an Italian military base is still active on La Maddalena, work has begun to convert the old military hospital and arsenal into hotels.

Italians voted to be annexed into the Kingdom of Sardinia, technically making Italy a part of Sardinia! Things began looking up for Sardinia in the late 19th century: the railway was completed in 1874, overseas trade re-emerged, educational funding increased and banks appeared, giving the Sardi access to credit for the first time.

20th century

The First World War saw Sardinians emerge as heroes of the young Italian nation, as the Brigata Sassari, an all-Sardinian brigade, fought valiantly on some of the war's most dangerous fronts. When they returned home, many brigade members played critical roles in forming the Partito Sardo d'Azione, whose central goal was greater control for the Sardi over their own affairs.

Mussolini promoted various agricultural schemes, designed to turn Sardinia's malarial wastelands into profitable pastures and although 75% of Cagliari suffered bombing damage during World War Two, the rest of Sardinia escaped largely unscathed. The island was finally granted a degree of autonomy in 1948, when it was given its own Regional Council and President. More importantly, the US-funded Rockefeller Foundation provided the DDT needed to eliminate malaria from the coastal regions in 1951, thus opening up areas that had been largely inaccessible and unproductive since Carthaginian times. The 1950s also saw Sardinia selected as one of Italy's underdeveloped zones in need of funding by the Cassa del Mezzogiorno, an ambitious, $2 billion programme designed to lift southern Italy from its economic inertia. Recently drained swamps that had formerly been malarial breeding grounds were given to peasants in 15-acre plots, and millions of dollars were targeted at creating artificial lakes to bolster the island's electricity generation and irrigation capacities.

However, despite these occasional government handouts, in many ways Sardinia remained a neglected, backwater colony for much of the late 20th century, receiving as few favours from Rome as it had under its previous rulers. A series of unproductive industrial schemes in the 1960-70s littered the island with sprawling petrochemical plants owned by outside interests that still funnel most of the profits off the island. Similarly, the Costa Smeralda, which was developed by the Aga Khan in 1962 may have put Sardinia on the worldwide map, but the coast's profits headed offshore. With more NATO bases per square kilometre than anywhere else on Earth, parts of the island resemble a remote dumping ground for the industrial and military ventures that Italy depends on but doesn't want to look at.

But there's hope on the horizon. As the island slowly awakens to its own natural beauty, tourism has grown steadily since mainland Italians first started coming in the 1950s and is helping to drag Sardinia out of its economic hibernation. A lack of industry caused 45% of Sardinia's population to move to larger cities or off the island between 1955 and '75 but emigration has since slowed and unemployment dipped under 10% in 2007 for the first time in the island's history. As this once remote colony drifts closer and closer to its neighbours, only time will tell whether the Sardi can manage to foster a future of economic sustainability without sacrificing their ancient, cultural roots.

Contents

Footnotes

Menu reader

General
affumicato smoked
al sangue rare
alla griglia grilled
antipasto starter/appetizer
arrosto roasted
ben cotto well done
bollito boiled
caldo hot
contorni side dishes
coppa/cono cup/cone
cotto cooked
cottura media medium
crudo raw
degustazione tasting menu of several dishes
dolce dessert
fatto in casa homemade
forno a legna wood-fired oven
freddo cold
fresco fresh
fritto fried
piccante spicy
primo first course
ripieno stuffed
secondo second course

Drinks (*bevande*)
acqua naturale/gassata/frizzante still/sparkling water
birra beer
birra (alla spina) beer (draught)
bottiglia bottle
caffè coffee (ie espresso)
caffè macchiato/ristretto espresso with a dash of foamed milk/strong
spremuta freshly squeezed fruit juice
succo juice
vino bianco/rosato/rosso white/rosé/red wine
vin santo a dark, sweet, fortified wine

Fruit (*frutta*) and vegetables (*verdure*)
agrumi citrus fruits
anguria watermelon
arance oranges
carciofio globe artichoke
castagne chestnuts
ciliegie cherries
cipolle onions
fagioli white beans
fichi figs
finocchio fennel
fragole strawberries
funghi mushrooms

lamponi raspberries
legumi pulses
lenticchie lentils
mandorla almond
melagrana pomegranate
melanzana eggplant/aubergine
melone melon
mele apples
noci walnuts
nocciole hazelnuts
patate potatoes, which can be *arroste* (roast), *fritte* (fried), *novelle* (new), *pure'di* (mashed)
peperoncino chilli pepper
peperone peppers
pesche peaches
pinoli pine nuts
piselli peas
pomodori tomatoes
rucola rocket
spinaci spinach
tartufi truffles
zucca pumpkin

Meat (*carne*)
affettati misti mixed cured meat
agnello lamb
bistecca beef steak
carpaccio finely sliced raw meat (usually beef)
cinghiale wild boar
coda alla vaccinara oxtail
coniglio rabbit
involtini thinly sliced meat, rolled and stuffed
lepre hare
manzo beef
pollo chicken
polpette meatballs
polpettone meat loaf
porchetta roasted, stuffed suckling pig
prosciutto ham – cotto cooked, crudo cured
salsicce pork sausage
salumi misti cured meats
speck a type of cured, smoked ham
spiedini meat pieces grilled on a skewer
stufato meat stew
trippa tripe
vitello veal

Fish (*pesce*) and seafood (*frutti di mare*)
acciughe anchovies
anguilla eel
aragosta lobster
baccalà salt cod
bottarga mullet-roe

branzino sea bass
calamari squid
cozze mussels
frittura di mare/frittura di paranza small fish, squid and
  shellfish lightly covered with flour and fried
frutti di mare seafood
gamberi shrimps/prawns
grigliata mista di pesce mixed grilled fish
orata gilt-head/sea bream
ostriche oysters
pesce spada swordfish
polpo octopus
sarde, sardine sardines
seppia cuttlefish
sogliola sole
spigola bass
stoccafisso stockfish
tonno tuna
triglia red mullet
trota trout
vongole clams

Dessert (*dolce*)
cornetto sweet croissant
crema custard
dolce dessert
gelato ice cream
granita flavoured crushed ice
macedonia (di frutta) fruit salad
panettone type of fruit bread eaten at Christmas
semifreddo a partially frozen dessert
sorbetto sorbet
tiramisù rich dessert with cake, cream,
  coffee and chocolate
torta cake
tozzetti sweet, crunchy almond biscuits
zabaglione whipped egg yolks flavoured with
  Marsala wine
zuppa inglese trifle

Other
aceto balsamico balsamic vinegar, always from Modena
arborio type of rice used to make risotto
burro butter
calzone folded pizza
formaggi misti mixed cheese plate
formaggio cheese
frittata omelette
insalata salad
insalata Caprese tomatoes, mozzarella and basil
latte milk
miele honey

olio oil
polenta cornmeal
pane bread
pane-integrale brown bread
panzanella bread and tomato salad
provola smoked cheese
ragù a meaty sauce or ragout
riso rice
salsa sauce
sugo sauce or gravy
strangozzi/strozzapreti a thick, Umbrian sort of
  spaghetti
umbricelli thick spaghetti
zuppa soup

Useful words and phrases
aperitivo a pre-dinner drink,
  often served with free snacks
posso avere il conto? can I have the bill please?
coperto cover charge
bicchiere glass
c'è un menù? is there a menu?
aperto/chiuso open/closed
prenotazione reservation
conto the bill
cameriere/cameriera waiter/waitress
che cosa mi consegna? what do you recommend?
cos'è questo? what's this?
dov'è il bagno? where's the toilet?

Index → *Entries in bold refer to maps.*